Confetti

The Kids' Make-It-Yourself, Do-It-Yourself Party Book

Confetti

The Kids' Make-It-Yourself, Do-It-Yourself Party Book

by Phyllis Fiarotta and Noel Fiarotta

WORKMAN PUBLISHING/NEW YORK

Library of Congress Cataloging in Publication Data

Fiarotta, Phyllis.
   Confetti: the kids' make-it-yourself,
   do-it-yourself party book

   SUMMARY: Instructions for twenty-two parties, including birthday, holiday, Mother's Day, and new baby, with details for making invitations, decorations, favors, and food.
   1. Handicraft — Juvenile literature.   2. Cookery — Juvenile literature.   3. Children's parties — Juvenile literature.   [1. Parties] I. Fiarotta, Noel, joint author. II.   Title.
TT160.F472   790.19'22   78-7121
ISBN 0-89480-049-3
ISBN 0-89480-050-7 pbk.

Book Design: Bernard Springsteel
Illustrations: Phyllis Fiarotta
Photographs: Ray Solowinski
Cover Design: Paul Hanson
Cover Photographs: Ray Solowinski

Workman Publishing
1 West 39 Street
New York, New York 10018

Manufactured in the United States of America
First Printing October 1978
10 9 8 7 6 5 4 3 2 1

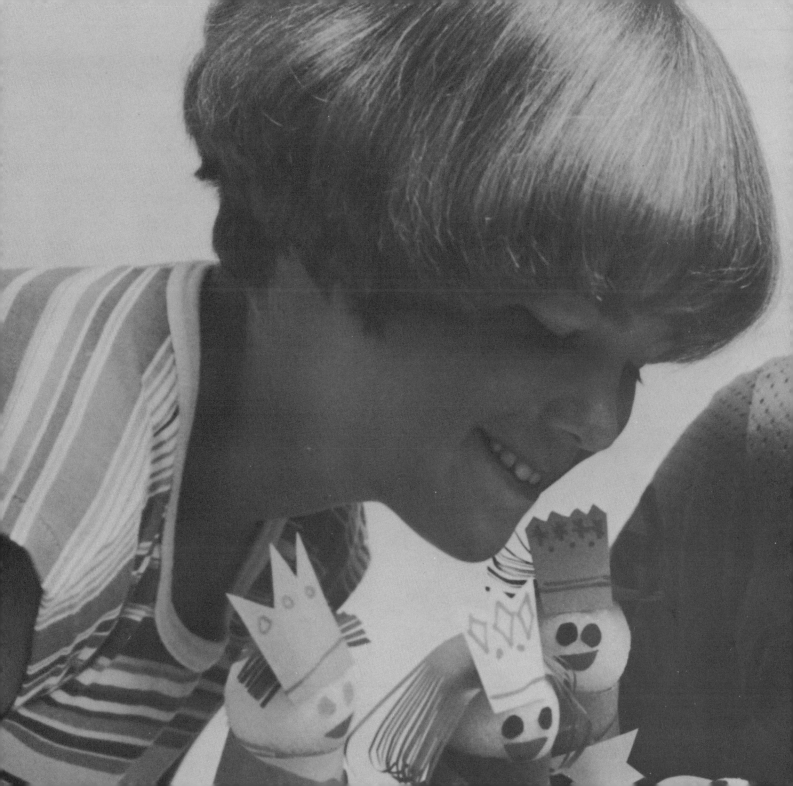

SYBIL PINCUS

LEE LULU

ALMA AND GENE DeFELIPPO

HOWARD AND
JOANN LaMARCA

KAREN RAJSTETER

ELIZABETH SPRINGSTEEL

BERNIE SPRINGSTEEL

TONY MANULI

MOTHER

ESTHER GINSBERG
(not pictured)

HENRY RUSSO
PETER LOOS
BARBARA PATTERSON
FATHER
CHARLIE MERRETS
FRED PATTERSON
JOAN BRENNAN
ED RAJSTETER
ELAINE RUSSO
MIKE CALDERARO
CAROL KEEFER
GEORGE LABIK
JOSEPH LULU

We dedicate this book to our good friends who are worth more to us than all the treasures of the world.

CHRIS BAKER

Contents

Holiday Parties

FOR THE ADULT

Why not make this the Year of the Party? Parties are fun times for children of all ages, but there never seems to be enough of them, although the calendar is filled with many scheduled holidays, special occasions, and, of course, annual birthdays.

A party doesn't have to be a large undertaking. The only requirement need be that your children derive pleasure from being with their family or friends in a festive atmosphere. *Confetti* contains birthday, holiday, and special occasion parties, but it is not only a party book. It is also a craft book with many projects that can be constructed and used as decorations as well as presents and holiday favors.

All the ingredients for fun are included; making invitations, cakes and other refreshments, decorations, party favors, and more. Many of the items can be made from kitchen throwaways (cardboard boxes and tubes, dairy cartons, tin cans) or your children's art and school supplies. There is very little you have to buy.

The Asterisk

If you feel that a task is too difficult for a child, offer assistance. Many projects take place in the kitchen, and you should be present when children are baking and handling kitchen utensils. A single asterisk — * — in front of a step signals we feel help is needed, but in all cases the child should feel he or she created the finished project.

You can be sure, that whenever this book is opened, whether for party suggestions or craft projects, a celebration of fun will begin.

JUST FOR YOU

Your birthday is your very own important occasion, but a birthday isn't the only time for a celebration. Thumb through this book, and you will find not only eight different kinds of birthday parties but also seven popular holiday parties and seven special occasion parties.

Check your calendar and see what special day is coming up soon. It might be your birthday, a favorite holiday, or an extra special occasion — like Mother's Day or Father's Day. If it is your birthday, choose one of the ethnic celebrations or the All-American Party. You can even mix and match parties for an international touch. Each holiday and special occasion, also includes everything you need for fun.

Once you're chosen a party, be sure you have enough time to prepare for it. There are many decorations to make, invitations to send, and foods to prepare. Read all the directions several times before you begin. Ask an adult for help if there is something you don't understand, but many times a careful look at the drawing is all you need.

You don't have to have a party to enjoy *Confetti*. There are so many crafts that you can make at any time of the year. But, if you are in the mood for a celebration, get started quickly.

CRAFT SUPPLIES

PAPER

● **White drawing paper** is important in many craft projects. It is heavy, smooth paper that comes in pads or packages.

● **Colored paper** is heavy paper that comes in many wonderful colors. The sheets are sold in packages, and many paper sizes are available. Save all large scraps in a box or bag for smaller projects.

- **Tracing paper** is very light and transparent. When it is placed on a drawing you can see the drawing through it. Tracing paper is sold in pads.

- **Typewriter paper** is a white paper that is lighter in weight than drawing paper, but heavier than tracing paper. It is sold in packages or pads.

- **Cardboard** is very heavy paper. You can find it tucked in shirts which come from the laundry or in packages of new clothes. A large supply of cardboard is available from cereal and detergent boxes, and other kitchen throwaways. Cardboard may also be bought in art supply stores.

- **Corrugated cardboard** is a brown cardboard that many cartons are made from. It is a sandwich of a ripply center paper glued between two sheets of heavy brown paper.

- **Poster board,** sometimes called oaktag, is a lightweight cardboard and is sold at stationery or art supply stores, and some five-and-tens. It is available in white as well as in a wide variety of colors and can be used in projects as a substitute for large colored paper.

- **Colored tissue paper** is lightweight paper that you can see through. It comes in many colors and is sold in packages at stationery or art supply stores, and in some five-and-tens. It is easy to fold and cut.

GLUES AND PASTE

- **White glue** comes in plastic bottles with applicator tips. This glue makes a strong bond when it dries.

- **Liquid brown glue,** or mucilage, comes in a bottle with a rubber cap that is used for spreading. It is a light adhesive.

- **Paper paste** is a thick adhesive. It usually comes in a jar and has a plastic spreader.

BAKING SUPPLIES

- **Cake pans** are needed for almost every party. The ones used in this book are round, round with a center tube (angel food cake), square, or cupcake size.

- **Boxed cake mixes** are the quickest and easiest way to make a cake. They come in different flavors and are used for all the different cakes in this book.

● **Frosting mixes** are sold in boxes and come in many different flavors. You can also use a canned ready-made frosting if you prefer.

● **Gel icings** are sold in small tubes. They come in colors and are used to add designs on cakes.

● **Other supplies** include mixing bowls and spoons, and measuring cups and spoons. These are used in preparing and baking your cake.

Note: We found that cake and icing mixes were easy to follow and baked up into good tasting treats. If you have a favorite cake recipe which you would rather use, then by all means use it to bake your party cake. Follow our decorating directions once the cake has cooled.

MISCELLANEOUS

● **Confetti** is easy to make. Just rip up colored paper into the tiniest pieces and put them into a bowl ready to throw when the time comes.

● **Compasses** are used to make a perfect circle. They have two arms, one pointed and one which holds a pencil. The compass opens and closes, and you can draw any size circle you need.

● **Paper punches** are used to make holes in paper and lightweight cardboard. These holes are the size of those punched in looseleaf paper. To make a hole, a piece of paper is inserted in the punch which is squeezed and released.

● **Cord** comes in many thicknesses and is usually white or a natural brown in color. Kite string is considered thin cord and rope is thick cord. Cord is available at stationery or hardware stores.

● **Colored markers** are tubes or "pencils" of enclosed ink with a felt coloring tip. There are two kinds of markers. Indelible markers do not wash out with water. Watercolor markers will smudge if they contact water.

● **Kitchen throwaways** are used in many projects in this book. They include round containers, square and rectangular boxes, tubes, tin cans, and dairy cartons. Save all throwaways for future projects.

● **Foam balls** are sold at flower shops, craft stores, and at Christmastime, at decoration counters. They come in one-, two- and three-inch sizes.

Birthday Parties

You had to be really important thousands of years ago to have a birthday party. In fact, the first known birthday celebration took place in ancient Egypt. It was given in honor of Pharoah, King of Egypt. Since you too are some-one special why not have a party on your birthday which is fit for a king? Celebrate with an international touch. Here are eight parties to choose from, each with a particular flavor all its own.

George Washington, Christopher Columbus, and *you* have one thing in common, a yearly birthday celebration. That's right, your birthday is just as important as the other two. This year, circle your special day on the calendar and plan to have a rip-roaring, All-American carnival party. Scatter plenty of balloons around the party room. In the center of the table place a delicious carrousel cake and alongside it, a jester filled with party favors, one for each guest. Give everyone a clown mask as well as a pointed pom-pom hat. Ice cream, popcorn balls, candy apples, and hot chocolate with melted marshmallows are all-time favorites. This party might just turn out to be "The Greatest Show on Earth."

All-American Party

Balloon Invitations

Send your party invitations
On a colorful balloon,
Make sure you tell your special friends
It's coming up real soon.

THINGS YOU NEED — scissors, colored paper, glue, crayons or markers

1. Cut a long piece of colored paper and fold it in half along the shorter side.
2. Cut circles from colored paper. Glue them to the front of the folded paper, as shown in the drawing.
3. Write the words, "It's a Birthday Party," on the circles with a crayon or marker.
4. Draw lines extending from the circles for balloon strings.
5. Write the party information on the inside.

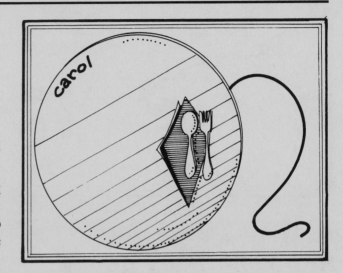

Balloon Place Mats

Serve your guests a party treat
On pretty mats, dig in and eat!

THINGS YOU NEED — colored paper, compass, scissors, yarn, tape, crayons or markers

1. Draw a large circle on colored paper with a compass. Cut it out.
2. Cut a length of yarn and tape it to the back of the circle.
3. Write the name of a guest near the edge of the circle with a crayon or marker.

Happy Birthday Hanger

Across the room for all to see,
Announce it bright and gay,
That all are here to celebrate,
On this your special day.

THINGS YOU NEED — scissors, colored paper, pencil, ruler, paper punch, string or yarn, tape

1. Cut thirteen rectangles from colored paper, all the same size.
2. Using a pencil and ruler, draw a letter on each to spell the words, "H • A • P • P • Y B • I • R • T • H • D • A • Y." The letters should be thick and fill up most of the paper, Fig. a.
3. Cut out the letters.
4. Punch two holes at the top of each letter with a paper punch, Fig. b.
5. Weave a very long piece of yarn or string in and out of the holes to spell "Happy Birthday," Fig. c.
6. Tape the greeting from one wall to another.

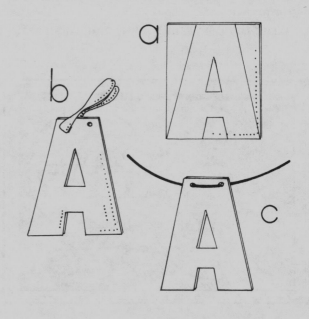

Clown Hats

Pointed hats with fringe on top
And pom-poms up and down
Make every party guest this day
A funny circus clown.

THINGS YOU NEED—large sheets of colored paper, tape, scissors, glue, stapler, ribbon

1. Roll a sheet of colored paper into a cone large enough to fit on your head.
2. Tape the cone in place, Fig. a.
3. Trim the bottom edge to make a circle. Cut a small opening at the top point.
4. Cut slits into one long side of a long, narrow strip of paper, Fig. b.
5. Roll the uncut edge of the slit paper around itself and tape it to form a tassel, Fig. c.
6. Push the end of the tassel into the hole on top of the hat, Fig. d.
7. Glue paper circles on the hat.
8. Staple two lengths of ribbon, opposite each other, inside the hat, Fig. e.

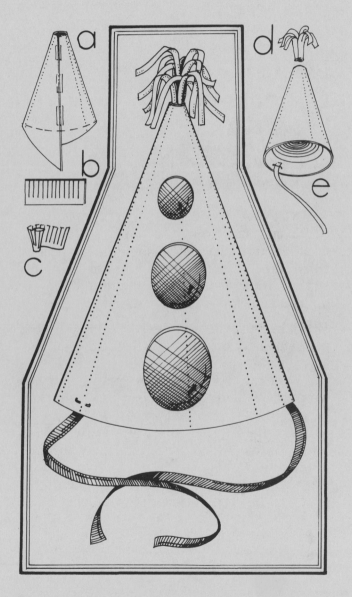

Carrousel Cake

Carrousels with horses and bells
Are fun to ride upon,
A carrousel cake is fun to bake
And eat until it's gone.

THINGS YOU NEED—cake mix, two round cake pans, plate, frosting mix, plastic knife, gel icing in a tube, scissors, colored paper, pencil, ruler, tape, paper punch, plastic drinking straws, toothpicks, regular marshmallows, miniature-size marshmallows.

*1. Bake a cake in two round cake pans. Follow package directions. Remove from the pans and let cool.

2. Place the cooled cakes on a plate. Or, if you want, place them on a cardboard circle that has been covered with aluminum foil.

3. Mix the frosting and frost between the layers. Spread the frosting on the top and sides of the cake with a plastic knife.

4.   Add a loop design around the sides of the cake near the top with gel icing in a tube, Fig. a.

5. Cut a sheet of colored paper much longer than it is wide. Mark the center point on the top edge with a pencil.

6. Draw lines from the center point to the bottom and sides of the paper with a ruler; study Fig. b.

7. Roll the paper into a wide cone and tape in place, Fig. c.

8. Trim the bottom edge of the cone to form a curve, Figs. c and d.

9. Make scalloped curved cuts along the rounded edge, from line to line, Fig. e.

10. Punch a hole in the center of every second or third scallop curve near the edge with a paper punch, Fig. f.

11. Push plastic drinking straws into the punched holes. Push the straws into the cake to form the roof, Fig. g.

12. Tape a small colored paper triangle to the flat end of a toothpick for a flag, Fig. h. Push the flag into the point of the roof.

13. Attach two regular-sized marshmallows together with a toothpick, Fig. i.

14. Attach two miniature marshmallows to one end of a toothpick, Fig. j. Make four.

15. Push the attached marshmallows into the regular marshmallows to make arms and legs, Fig. k.

16. Place several marshmallow figures on the cake under the roof of the carrousel.

17. Roll, tape, and trim cone hats for the marshmallow figures, Fig. l. Attach the hats to the heads with a dab of gel icing.

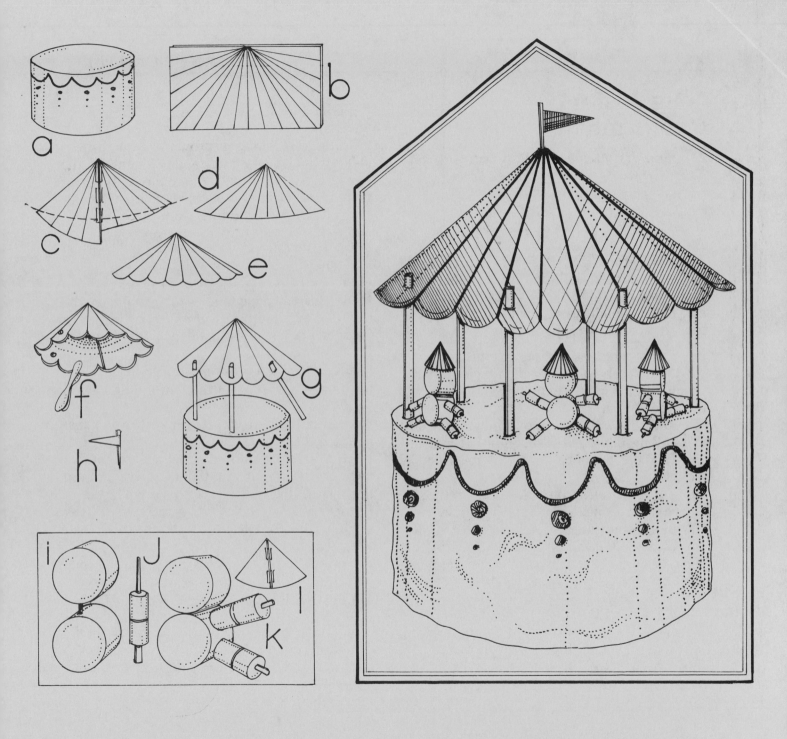

Jolly Jester Centerpiece

At your party all guests are excited,
To have a young jester invited.
He's the centerpiece treat,
And has candy to eat,
Making all of your friends quite delighted.

THINGS YOU NEED—scissors, colored paper, cardboard bathroom tissue tube, tape, Ping-Pong ball, glue, white tissue paper, markers, paper punch, yarn, quart-sized milk carton, rock, small wrapped favors.

1. Cut a piece of paper as high as the cardboard tube and long enough to wrap around it plus a little extra. Tape the paper to the tube, Fig. a.

2. Roll colored paper into a cone that will fit over a Ping-Pong ball. Tape in place, Fig. b.

3. Trim the bottom edge of the cone to make a circle, Fig. c.

4. Cut two circles from colored paper the size of the Ping-Pong ball. Cut the circles into half-moon shapes; see dotted line in Fig. d.

5. Glue the half-moons to the cone, Fig. e.

6. Cut several squares of white tissue paper large enough to wrap around a Ping-Pong ball plus a little extra.

7. Place the Ping-Pong ball in the center of the stacked tissue. Bring the sides up over the ball and twist them together, Figs. f and g.

8. Draw a face on the tissue-covered ball with a marker.

9. Glue the cone to the ball, with the ends of the tissue tucked inside, Fig. h.

10. Cut a very long, narrow rectangle for the collar. Fold it evenly back and forth until all the paper is used up, Fig. i. Make the folds small.

11. Open the paper. Punch a hole in the center of each folded section near one edge, Fig. j.

12. Weave a length of yarn in and out of the holes to form the collar, Fig. k. Even up the yarn ends.

13. Glue the head to the top of the tube, Fig. l.

14. Glue small paper circles to the points of the half-moons, glue paper arms to both sides of the tube near the head, and add paper buttons, Fig. m.

15. Tie the folded collar under the head, Fig. n.

16. Cut off the bottom third of a milk carton with a scissors.

17. Cover the bottom section with paper just as you did the tube, Fig. o.

18. Cut a J from colored paper and glue it to a different-colored paper. Glue it to the front of the carton, Fig. p.

19. Push a rock into the bottom of the cardboard tube. Place the jester inside the carton, Fig. q.

20. Cut long pieces of yarn, one for each guest. Knot all the yarn together at one end. Tie each of the other ends to a small, wrapped favor.

21. Place the jester centerpiece on the table. Push the tied ends of yarn into the carton in front of the jester. Place one favor near each place setting.

Carnival Gifts

No party is complete without
A gift for every guest.
Place each in a cardboard box,
All wrapped to look their best.

THINGS YOU NEED — scissors, white or brown wrapping paper, crayons or markers, gift in a box, tape, ribbon

1. Cut the paper long enough to wrap around the box plus a little extra. The sides should overlap a little more than half the height of the box, Fig. a.
2. Draw balloon designs on the wrapping paper with crayons or markers.
3. Wrap the paper around the box and tape in place, Fig. b. The sides should overlap the box equally on both ends.
4. Fold in the left and right sides of the paper on one end of the box and tape, Fig. c. Crease the top and bottom remaining paper into points.
5. Fold the top point down and tape, Fig. d.
6. Fold the bottom point up and tape, Fig. e.
7. Do the same on the other side of the box.
8. Turn the box upside down so the seam is on the bottom.
9. Cut a very long piece of ribbon. Place the

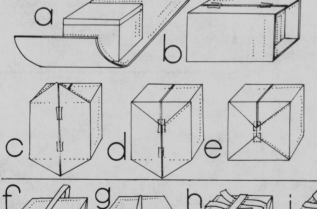

center of the ribbon over the top of the box, Fig. f.

10. Bring the ends under the box and twist, Fig. g.

11. Bring the ends to the top of the box and under the ribbon, Fig. h.

12. Tie the ends into a knot, Fig. i.

13. Fold a length of ribbon back and forth three times to make two loops, Fig. j.

14. Place the looped ribbon over the knot on the box, Fig. k.

15. Tie tightly to form a bow, Fig. 1.

Pin the Nose on Rose

There once was a cute clown named Rose,
Who was missing —what do you suppose?
Each guest she would call,
Eyes shut, to the wall
Where she hung waiting for a new nose.

THINGS YOU NEED —scissors, colored paper, glue, large sheets of paper, crayons or markers, tape

1. Study the drawing then cut out a face, hat, hair, eyes, cheeks, collar, bow tie, and flower from colored paper.

2. Glue all of the clown features on a large paper circle.

3. Draw a big smile on the clown's face with a crayon or marker and an X where the nose should be.

4. Cut paper circles for noses.

5. To play the game, blindfold a player and give him or her a nose with a piece of tape attached to it. Spin the player around three times and aim him or her towards the clown. The player whose nose lands closest to the X wins a prize.

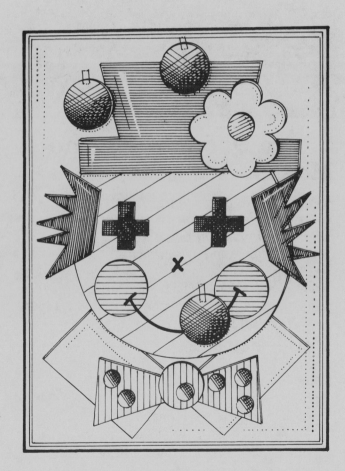

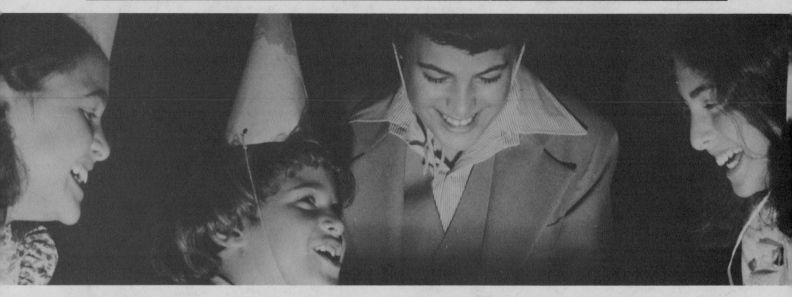

Clown Decorations and Masks

As masks and decorations,
Make funny circus clowns.
Each friend gets a different face —
Some smiling, some with frowns.

THINGS YOU NEED—scissors, colored paper, glue, stapler, crayons or markers, tape, pencil, cotton balls, yarn.

A. Clown Decorations
1. Cut a large oval or circle head, Fig. a, a triangle hat, Fig. b, and an oval collar with a scalloped edge, Fig. c.
2. Glue the hat to the front of the head and the collar to the back of the head, Fig. d.
3. Study the drawing and cut hat buttons, eyes, nose, and cheeks from colored paper. Glue them on the face. Cut hair from yarn and staple it to the face.
4. Draw eyebrows and a mouth with crayons or markers.
5. Tape the clowns around the party room.

B. Clown Mask
1. Cut a large oval or circle, just as you did for clown decorations. It should fit on your face.
2. Place the paper in front of your face and mark where your eyes and mouth are with a pencil.
3. Cut a circle around the pencil marks.
4. Glue cotton balls to the hat. Staple yarn hair to each side of the hat. Make eye and mouth lines with a marker.
5. Staple one end of a length of ribbon to each side of the mask at the back, Fig. d.

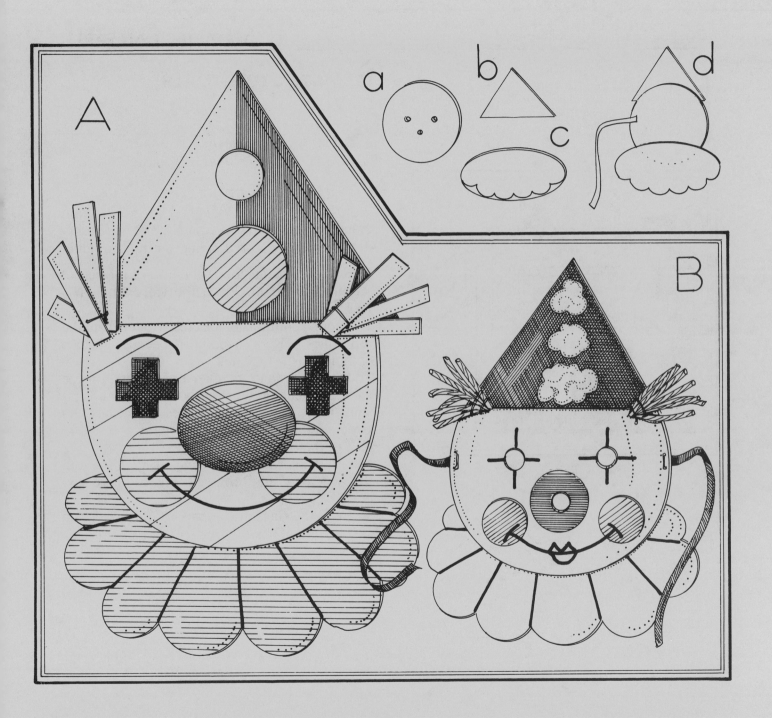

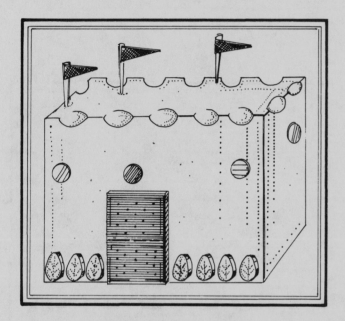

Ice Cream Castle

Here's a castle not of stone,
But really out-of-sight,
It has no king, no queen, no throne.
An ice cream lover's delight.

THINGS YOU NEED — half-gallon brick of vanilla ice cream, plate, spoon, graham cracker, spearmint-leaf candies, flat wafer candies, scissors, colored paper, toothpicks, glue

1. Remove the carton from around a brick of vanilla ice cream. Place the ice cream on a large plate.
2. Scoop spoonfuls of ice cream away from the top edges, Fig. a. Work fast because the ice cream will start to melt.
3. Press a graham cracker drawbridge on the ice cream centered at the bottom of one large side. Press in spearmint leaves for bushes and wafer candies for windows, Fig. b.
4. Put the castle into the freezer.
5. Cut a colored paper triangle flag. Glue it to the wide end of a toothpick, Fig. c. Make several.
6. Push the flags into the top of the ice-cream castle while it's in the freezer or just before it's served.

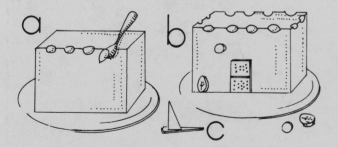

The Crunchiest Buttered Popcorn

Popcorn fresh with melted butter
Placed by every seat,
Crackly sounds your guests will utter,
Munching on this treat.

THINGS YOU NEED — popping corn, cooking oil, pot with cover, butter, salt, plastic sandwich bags, ribbon or yarn

1. Pop popping corn in oil in a covered pot. Follow package directions.
2. Pour melted butter over the popped corn and mix. Sprinkle with salt.
3. Put popcorn into plastic sandwich bags. Tie the bags closed with ribbon or yarn.

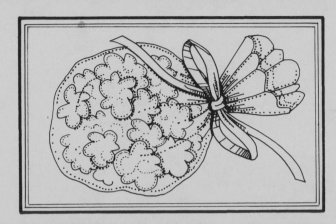

Candy Coated Apples

Crunchy apples on a stick,
Dipped in melted candy,
One for each will do the trick,
A snack so fine and dandy.

THINGS YOU NEED — package of red candy apple coating mix or a package of caramels, cooking pot, candy apple sticks, apples, plastic dish, waxed paper

*1. To make the coating, follow directions on a package of red candy apple mix or melt caramels in a pot (or a double-boiler) over very low heat on the stove.
2. Push a stick into the top of an apple.

3. Dip the apple into the melted candy mixture, covering it completely, Fig. a.
4. Remove and allow the excess melted candy to drip into a plastic dish, Fig. b. Make many.
5. Place apples on a sheet of waxed paper with the sticks facing up, Fig. c.

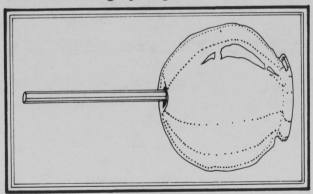

Little Added Extras

A. Booby Prize Balloons

1. Draw an X on many small pieces of paper. Draw an O on only one piece of paper.
2. Fold all the papers into tiny pieces. Push one into each balloon opening.
3. Blow up the balloons and knot the necks.
4. Give each guest a balloon to break. The guest with the O is the booby and gets a prize.

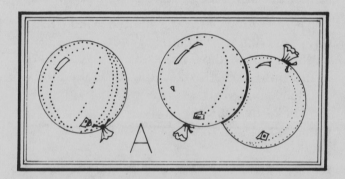

B. Hot Chocolate and Friends

Make hot chocolate to serve with the cake. Add miniature marshmallows.

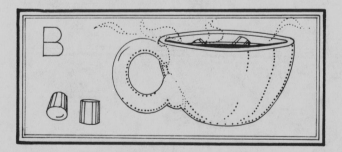

C. Wishing-Well Giftdrop

1. Find a large carton at your local supermarket.
2. Cut paper to fit on the sides.
3. Draw a brick design on the cut paper with a crayon and a ruler.
4. Tape or glue the paper to the sides of the carton.

5. Cut a black paper bucket shape, similiar to the one shown in the drawing, and tape it to the well.
6. Have your guests drop their gifts into the well when they arrive at your party.

And don't forget the confetti!

German Rootbeerfest Party

One colorful autumn day, in 1810, King Ludwig of Germany was married. He wanted everyone to share in his happiness. The wedding day was declared a time of fun and merrymaking for all. Ever since, German people celebrate Ludwig's happy event yearly and it is now known as Oktoberfest.

Oktoberfest takes place in the fall. People dress in festive costumes and gather in a park, or in someone's home or at the fairgrounds. They sing, dance, and feast on sausages, Bavarian beer and crunchy caraway-seed buns. People greet each other with a friendly "Guten Tag" (Hello).

A Rootbeerfest Birthday Party is just as exciting as this autumn holiday. Make believe your home is a German garden. Invite all of your friends for fine food and fun, just as King Ludwig did. Play stacks of records for dancing and singing. Make a Burgomaster centerpiece. (In towns in Germany, the Burgomaster is an important government official.) Most of all, have plenty of rootbeer on the table for everyone to drink.

Stein Place Mats

Your place mats have the right design —
For your fest, a rootbeer stein!

THINGS YOU NEED — pencil, large sheets of colored paper, scissors, white paper, glue, crayons or markers

1. Draw a rootbeer stein on a large sheet of colored paper, similar to the one shown in the drawing.
2. Cut out the stein.
3. Cut a shape from white paper that looks like

Stein Invitations

Grab your pen and write your best,
"Please Come to a ROOTBEERFEST."

THINGS YOU NEED — colored paper, pencil, scissors, glue, crayons or markers

1. Fold a long piece of colored paper in half.
2. Draw a stein (a mug) shape on the front of the folded paper, similar to the one shown in the drawing. The fold is at the top of the stein.
3. Cut out the stein through both layers of paper. Do not cut along the folded edge.
4. Write the words, "Come to a ROOTBEER-FEST," on the front of the stein. Write the information on the inside with a crayon or marker.

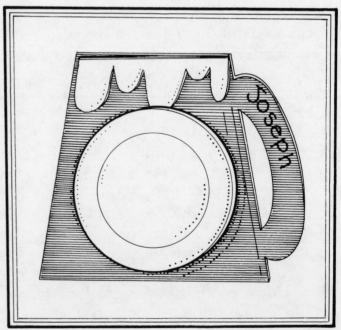

dripping rootbeer foam. It should fit across the top of the stein.

4. Glue the foam shape to the top of the stein.

5. Write the name of a guest on the handle with a crayon or marker.

Trailing Wiener Decorations

A rope of paper hot dogs,
Tied tightly one by one,
Hung high above the table,
Adds to the party fun.

THINGS YOU NEED — scissors, newspaper, brown tissue paper or crepe paper, string, yarn

1. Cut newspaper into confetti-sized pieces.

2. Cut several rectangles of brown colored tissue or crepe paper, all the same size.

3. Place a handful of newspaper confetti on a rectangle near one edge, Fig. a.

4. Roll the rectangle around the confetti newspaper, Fig. b.

5. Tie both ends tightly with string, Fig. c.

6. Tie the ends of the wieners together with yarn, Fig. d.

7. Make long ropes of wieners and decorate the party room with them.

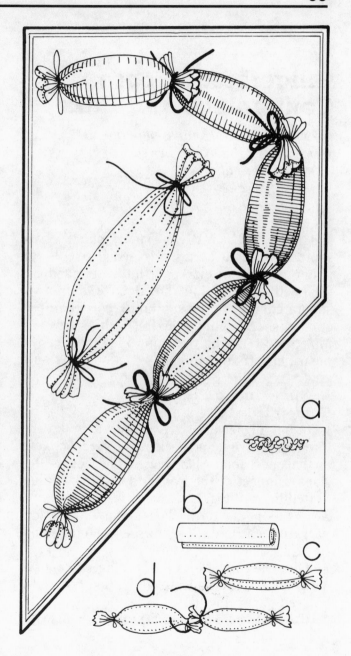

Gingerbread House Centerpiece and Cake

For your party you should plan ahead,
Your guests will have to be fed,
Get busy and bake
A one-story cake,
A house made of iced gingerbread.

THINGS YOU NEED—ruler, pencil, two same-sized cereal boxes, scissors, glue, colored paper, crayons or markers, flat wafer candies, wrapped favors, gingerbread cake mix, two square cake pans, plastic knife, cardboard or cookie sheet, aluminum foil, white frosting mix, food coloring, gel icing in a tube, jelly-beans, spearmint-leaf candy

A. Gingerbread House Centerpiece

1. Using a ruler draw a same-sized peak centered on the front and back of two cereal boxes, at the open end. Also draw a line across the sides, connecting the front and back peaks; see dotted lines in Fig. a.
2. Cut along the drawn lines, removing the top part from each box, Fig. b; see shaded area in Fig. a.
3. Glue the two boxes together, Fig. c. Let dry.
4. Trace the four sides of the glued boxes on colored paper, Fig. d.
5. Cut out the tracings. Decorate them with windows, doors, flowers, and gingerbread designs, using crayons or markers, Fig. e. You can glue on candies as part of the design.
6. Glue the decorated papers to the sides of the boxes, Fig. f.
7. Fold a piece of colored paper in half, Fig. g. It should be large enough to fit over the peak of the house. Fill the house with small, wrapped gifts as favors for each guest.

B. Gingerbread House Cake

1. Bake a cake in two square pans. Follow package directions. Remove from the pans and let cool.
2. Cut one cake in half, from corner to corner, on a diagonal, Fig. h.
3. Place the uncut cake on a piece of cardboard or a cookie sheet covered with aluminum foil. Place the two cut sections of cake together against the uncut cake to form the triangle roof, Fig. i.
4. Mix the frosting, following package directions. Color half of the frosting with red food coloring.
5. Cover the roof of the cake with red frosting and the house with white frosting, using a plastic knife.
6. Make windows with gel icing in a tube.
7. Decorate the roof with jellybeans. Add spearmint-leaf candy bushes and flat wafer candy decorations.

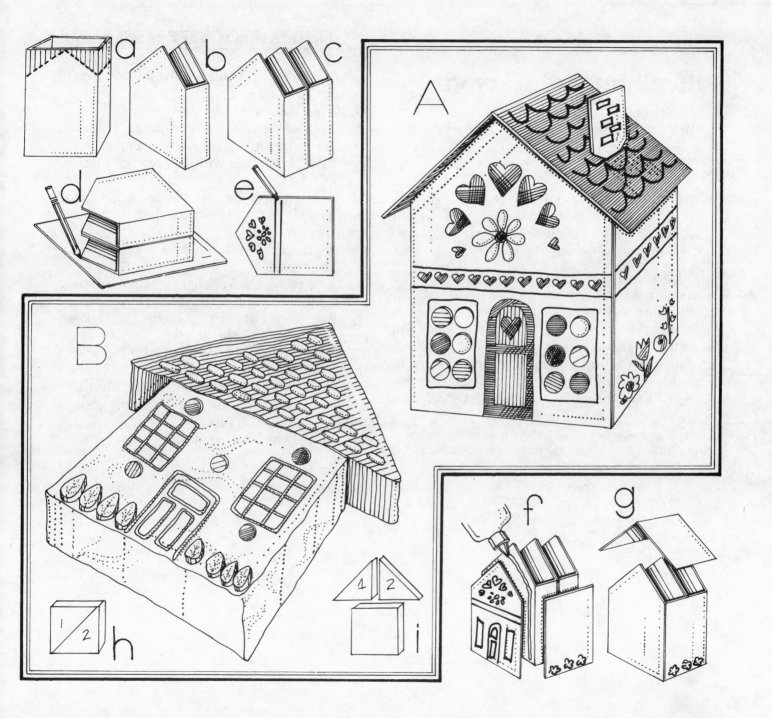

a

b

c

d

e

A

B

f

g

h

i

1
2

1 2

Rootbeer Stein Favors

Fill this mug
With favorite sweets.
Your guests will love
These party treats.

THINGS YOU NEED — colored paper, crayons or markers, tape, scissors, lightweight cardboard, pencil, glue, paper punch, yarn, candies

1. Draw a ribbon bow in the center of a piece of colored paper with a crayon or marker.
2. Roll the paper so that the top opening is smaller than the bottom opening. The sides will slant out. Tape in place, Fig. a.
3. Trim the top and bottom edges to form circles, Fig. a. The paper should stand, Fig. b.
4. Cut slits close together along the edge of the larger opening, Fig. c.
5. Fold the slit edge in to form tabs, Fig. d.
6. Place the large opening on a piece of light-weight cardboard. Trace around it with a pencil, Fig. e. Cut out circle.
7. Glue the circle to the tabs, Fig. f.
8. Cut a circle from colored paper. It should be slightly larger than the top opening of the stein. Draw a design with a crayon or marker, Fig. g.
9. Punch a hole near the edge of the circle with a paper punch. Punch a hole into the stein near the top edge.
10. Tie the circle to the stein with a small piece of yarn, Fig. h.
11. Cut a rectangle from lightweight cardboard about half the height of the stein. Draw a handle shape on the cardboard, as shown in the drawing, Fig. i. Cut out the handle.
12. Place the ends of the handle on the side of the stein. Mark the places where the handles touch the stein with a pencil, Fig. j.
13. Make slits along the lines. Slip the ends of the handle into the slits.
14. Fill the stein with candies.

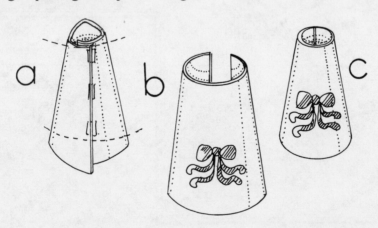

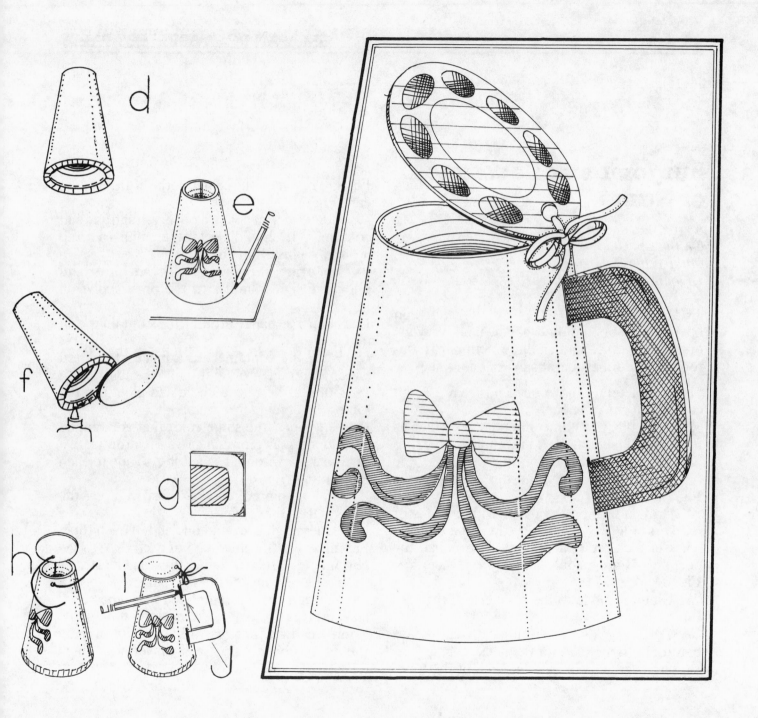

Burgomaster Decoration or Game

As a game or centerpiece,
On this special day,
Make a burgomaster,
To join in on the play.

THINGS YOU NEED—small tin can, can opener, scissors, colored paper, tape, crayons or markers, glue, feather, three cardboard bathroom tissue tubes, cardboard salt container

*1. Completely remove one end from a small can with a can opener.

2. Cut a piece of skin-colored paper as high as the can. It should be long enough to wrap around it plus a little extra, Fig. a.

3. Wrap the paper around the can and tape, Fig. b.

4. Draw a face on the paper with crayons or markers, Fig. c. The closed end is the bottom.

5. Cut a colored paper circle larger than the opening of the can for a hat. Glue a feather on it, Fig. d.

6. Glue the circle to the open end of the can, Fig. e.

*7. Cut away a small section of a cardboard bathroom tissue tube for the neck, Fig. f.

8. Squeeze glue around one end of the tube,

Fig. g. Press it on the center of the bottom of the can, Fig. h.

9. Cut a piece of colored paper as high as a salt container. It should be long enough to wrap around it plus a little extra.

10. Decorate the paper with cut-outs and crayon designs, similar to the ones shown in Fig. i.

11. Wrap the paper around the container and tape.

12. Place the container on a piece of colored paper and trace around it with a pencil, Fig. j.

13. Cut out the traced circle and glue it to the top of the container.

14. Cut paper (the same color that is wrapped around the salt container) to fit around two cardboard bathroom tissue tubes. Tape to each tube, Fig. k.

15. Glue a thin colored paper strip along the side of each tube, Fig. 1.

16. Squeeze glue around one end of each tube, Fig. m. Press the glued end of each tube to the bottom of the salt container, Fig. n. The stripes should be on the sides facing out.

17. You can use the completed burgomaster as a decoration. To play a game, stand him on the floor. Each player tries to knock him over by rolling a rubber ball. Each player gets three turns.

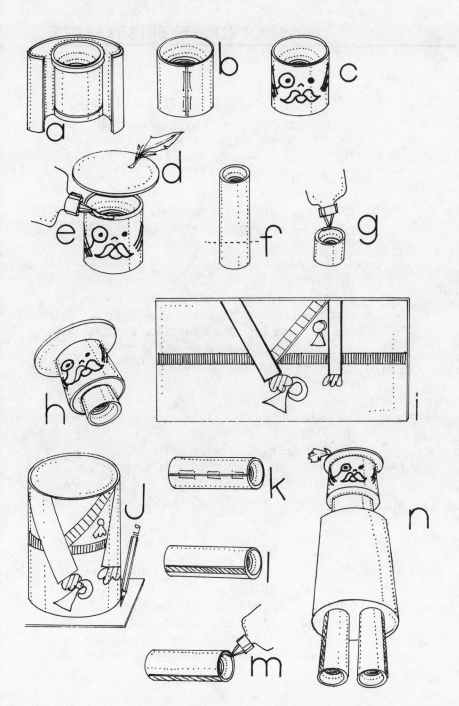

a

b

c

d

e

f

g

h

i

J

k

l

m

n

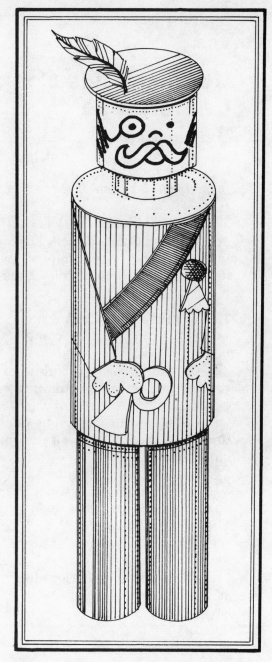

Harvest Juice Cask Centerpiece

Casks are little barrels,
And are made in different shapes.
Make one for a centerpiece
topped with a bunch of grapes.

THINGS YOU NEED — scissors, two sheets of poster board (oaktag), pencil, ruler, crayons or markers, tape, glue, colored paper, plastic drinking straw, cotton, colored tissue paper or crepe paper, pipe cleaners

A. Harvest Juice Cask

1. Cut a very long rectangle from poster board.
2. Draw a line across both long sides of the rectangle, a little way from the edges. Use a pencil and a ruler; see arrows in Fig. a.
3. Cut slits into both long sides, up to the drawn lines; see arrows Fig. a. They should be close together.
4. Draw lines up and down across the width with a crayon or marker and a ruler, Fig. a. The space between the lines should be no wider than your thumb.
5. Draw short lines scattered inside the spaces. Draw two circles on both sides of each short line. The lines will look like strips of wood held together with nails.
6. Roll the paper into a cylinder and tape, Fig. b.

7. Place the cylinder on half a sheet of poster board. Trace around it with a pencil, Fig. c.
8. Cut out the traced circle. Use it to trace and cut out another poster board circle.
9. Fold the slit ends of the cylinder toward the center to form tabs, Fig. d.
10. Make a hole in one circle, near the edge, with a sharp pencil, using a twisting motion, Fig. e.
11. Glue the circles to the tabs at both ends of the cylinder, Fig. f.
12. Glue two narrow, dark paper strips around the cylinder, close to the ends, Fig. g. You may have to glue two strips together to make them long enough to wrap around the cylinder.
13. Push a drinking straw into the hole in the circle, Fig. h.

B. Grapes

1. Place a small ball of cotton on a small grape colored square of tissue or crepe paper, Fig. i.
2. Gather up the sides, Fig. j. Fasten tightly with one end of a pipe cleaner, Fig. k. Make many.
3. Twist the pipe cleaner ends together to make a large cluster, Fig. l.
4. Draw leaf shapes on green paper rectangles. Draw a vein design on each leaf with a crayon or marker, Fig. m. Cut out the leaves.
5. Glue several leaves to the cluster of grapes.
6. Lay the cluster of grapes on top of the cask. They should remain in place without any glue.

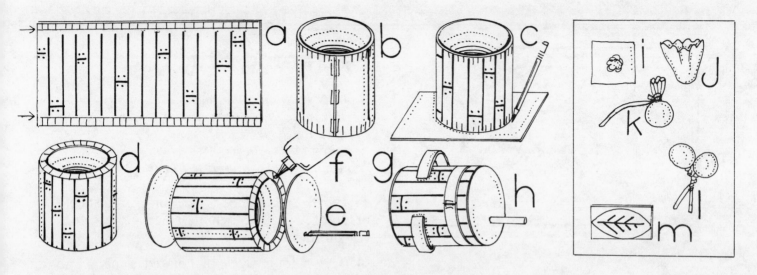

a b c

d f g h

e

i J k l m

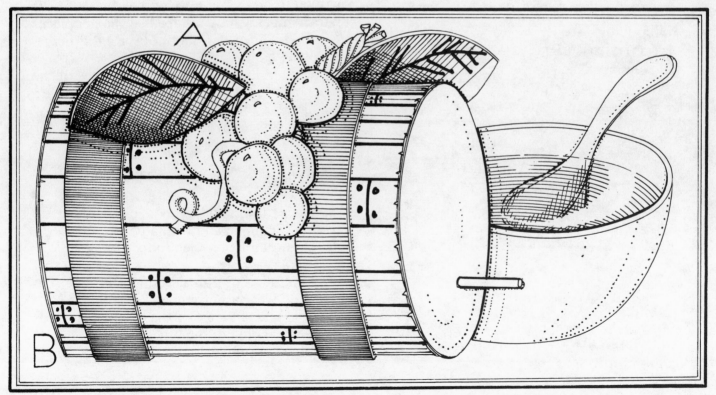

A

B

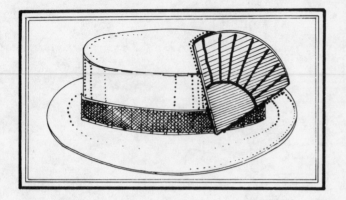

Feathered Hat

A clever hat maker named Flora,
So charming her friends all adore her,
Created her best,
For each party guest,
A hat called a feathered fedora.

THINGS YOU NEED — scissors, large sheets of colored paper, pencil, ruler, tape, glue, crayons or markers

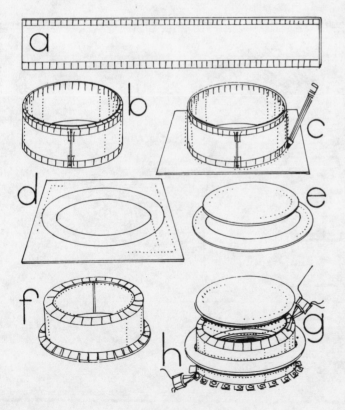

1. Cut a long piece of colored paper large enough to wrap around your head plus a little extra. You may have to tape two smaller pieces together. The paper should be a little higher than your hand.

2. Draw a line across both long sides of the paper, a little way from the edges, Fig. a. Use a pencil and a ruler.

3. Cut slits into each long side, up to the drawn lines, Fig. a. The slits should be close to each other.

4. Roll the paper into a cylinder and tape, Fig. b.

5. Place the cylinder on a piece of paper. Trace around one end with a pencil, Fig. c.

6. Draw another circle around the first circle to form a ring, Fig. d.

7. Carefully cut out the outer and inner circles. You will have a ring and a circle, Fig. e.

8. Fold one slit edge of the cylinder towards the center. Fold out the other slit edge, Fig. f.

9. Glue the circle to the tabs that face in, Fig. g.

10. Fit the ring over the cylinder for the hat's brim. Glue the ring on the tabs that stick out, Fig. h.

11. Cut a long paper hat band. Glue it around the hat, resting it on the brim. Cut a feather from colored paper and draw a design on it with a crayon or marker. Glue it to the hat band.

Winged Hat

A bird has wings,
So does a bat.
You can have wings—
Put on this hat.

THINGS YOU NEED—poster paint, brush, plastic food tub (from margarine) or plastic soup bowl, kitchen cleanser, scissors, ribbon, stapler, pencil

1. Paint a plastic food tub, if it has writing on it, with poster paint. A little kitchen cleanser added to the paint helps it stick to the plastic.

2. Staple two lengths of ribbon, opposite each other, on the inside of the tub, Fig. a.

3. Draw a wing shape on two paper rectangles, Fig. b.

4. Cut out the wings.

5. Staple the wings above each ribbon on the outside of the tub, Fig. c.

Horse and Rider Ring Toss

Each person gets three rings to throw
At the rider and the horse.
The player who loops all three rings
Wins the game, of course.

THINGS YOU NEED—corrugated cardboard, compass, pencil, scissors, crayons or markers, poster paints, brush, yarn, glue, colored paper, toothpick, plastic drinking straws, beads, plastic rings from a six-pack of canned beverage, cardboard

*1. Draw a large circle on a piece of corrugated cardboard with a compass. Cut out the circle.
*2. Draw two lines across the circle, equally spaced from the center (compass point), Fig. a.
3. Cut along the drawn lines to form two rockers.
4. Paint the rockers with poster paint. Decorate them with a crayon or marker, Fig. b.
5. Cut a small corrugated cardboard rectangle for the rider's body. Draw lines from the bottom corners to the top edge, as shown in Fig. c.
6. Cut another rectangle narrower and much longer than the first for the horse's head. Draw the design similar to the one shown in Fig. d.
*7. Cut out the body and head with a scissors (light areas in Figs. c and d). Paint.

8. Draw a face on the horse with crayon or marker. Cut two ears from colored paper. Glue them to the top of the horse's head, Fig. e.
9. Cut small pieces of yarn for a mane. Glue them along the back of the horse's head, Fig. e.
*10. Cut a narrow and long cardboard rectangle for the tail that is even narrower and shorter than the horse's head.
11. Draw a tail shape on the rectangle, similar to the one shown in the drawing, Fig. f. Cut out and paint.
12. Cut two small paper circles for the rider's head. Draw hair and a face in profile on each.
13. Glue the wide end of a flat toothpick between the two head shapes, Fig. g.
14. Cut two pieces of a drinking straw for the rider's arms. Glue a bead to the end of each piece, Fig. h.
15. Glue the horse's head, the rider's body, and the horse's tail to the straight side of one rocker; study Fig. i.
16. Glue the other rocker over the first with the head, body, and tail between them.
17. Push the toothpick of the head into the top of the body shape. Glue the arms to each side of the body.
18. To play the game, each player gets three plastic rings or rings cut from cardboard. Rock the horse gently. The player throws the rings, trying to loop them over the rider's head.

Little Added Extras

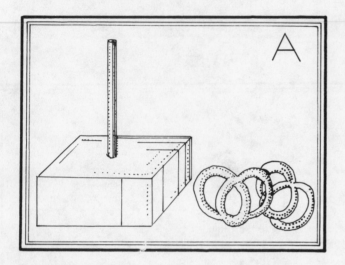

A. Pretzel Toss

1. Paint or cover a small cardboard box with paper.
2. Make a hole in the center of the top of the box with a sharp pencil, using a twisting motion.
3. Push a plastic drinking straw into the hole.
4. Each player gets several thin, twisted pretzels to toss at the straw from a measured distance. The winner gets to eat all the pretzels. If no one wins, divide the pretzels and start again.

B. Wunderbar Treats

1. Serve frothy rootbeer in paper cups with handles.
2. Serve bowls of grapes, if in season.
3. Have plenty of pretzels on hand.

C. Music

Everyone sings at the Oktoberfest. Play records and sing-along with all your guests.

And don't forget the confetti!

Japanese Doll and Kite Party

The children of Japan have their own special holiday called "Children's Day." It is a time for eating and having fun.

On this day the girls celebrate with a "Japanese Dolls Festival." Family dolls are taken out and displayed on shelves. The Emperor and Empress dolls sit on the top shelf. Next come the ministers and

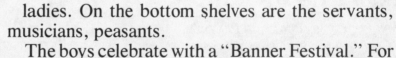

ladies. On the bottom shelves are the servants, musicians, peasants.

The boys celebrate with a "Banner Festival." For each boy in a family, a carp-fish banner is flown. Boys, too, display dolls. Soldiers, favorite heroes, and make-believe characters are some of the popular ones.

A Japanese birthday party can be lots of fun. Make the traditional Japanese dolls and instead of banners, make some really special kites to fly. Imagine flying one shaped like a huge house or a fat fish! A teahouse cake and a flower tower are just some of the decorations. When your guests arrive, they will think your party is taking place in Japan.

Fish Kite Place Mats

On lovely fish-shaped place mats,
Put the party food.
They make the table pretty,
And set the festive mood.

THINGS YOU NEED — scissors, large sheets of colored paper, white paper, crayons or markers, glue

1. Cut a large sheet of colored paper into a fish shape, similar to the one shown in the drawing.
2. Cut a circle from white paper and draw an eye in the center with a crayon or marker. Write the name of a guest around the eye.
3. Glue the eye to the fish. Draw on fish scales.

Fish Kite Invitations

Send party greetings on this fish,
"Come to my party," is your wish.

THINGS YOU NEED — pink or red paper, pencil, scissors, crayons or markers

1. Fold a long piece of pink or red paper in half along the shorter side.
2. Draw a fish design on one side, similar to the one shown in the drawing. The tail is at the open end.
3. Cut out the fish through both layers of paper. Do not cut along the folded edge.
4. Write your announcement on the outside and the party information on the inside with a crayon or marker.

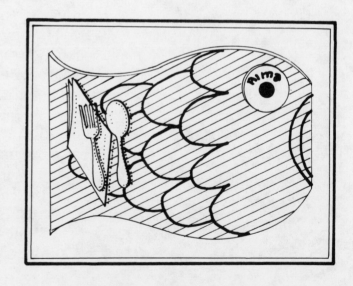

Teahouse Cake

For this birthday party you'll make,
A taste treat that's good fun to bake,
You'll serve it with pride,
With a tree on each side,
It's a Japanese teahouse-shaped cake.

THINGS YOU NEED—cake mix, two square cake pans, plastic knife, cookie sheet, aluminum foil, white frosting mix, food coloring

*1. Bake a cake in two square pans. Follow package directions. Remove from the pans and let cool.

*2. Cut one cake, following the diagram in Fig. a. Cover a cookie sheet with aluminum foil. Arrange the cut cake and the uncut cake on the cookie sheet, as shown in Fig. b. All sides of the cake should be touching.

3. Mix the white frosting, following package directions.

4. Divide the frosting into three equal parts. Add red food coloring to one part and green to a second part.

5. Spread red frosting on the roof, white on the house, and green on the bushes with a plastic knife.

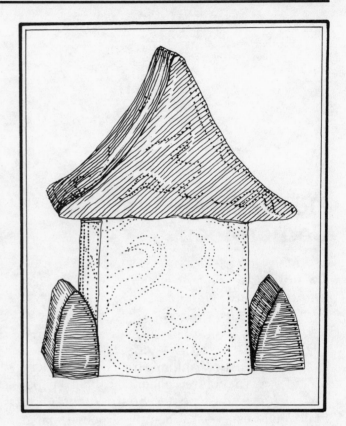

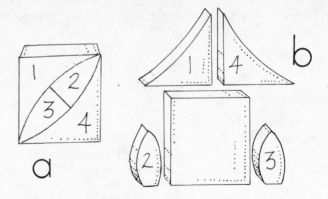

Flower Tower Centerpiece

In Japan on party day,
The host makes paper flowers,
And stacks them high for all to see.
In pretty rounded towers.

THINGS YOU NEED—scissors, colored tissue paper, plastic drinking straws, embroidery thread or yarn, colored paper, cardboard paper towel tube, tape, poster board (oaktag) or lightweight cardboard, compass, pencil, paper punch, deep cardboard box

1. Cut a long strip from colored tissue paper. Cut slits along one long side, Fig. a.
2. Wrap the uncut side around a plastic drinking straw to form a flower, Fig. b.
3. Tie the tissue paper tightly to the straw with colored embroidery thread or yarn, Fig. c. Make sixteen flowers.
4. Cut a piece of colored paper as high as a cardboard paper towel tube and long enough to wrap around it plus a little extra, Fig. d.

5. Wrap the paper around and tape, Fig. e.
6. Draw two large circles with a compass on poster board. Trace one end of the tube, centered, on each, Fig. f.
7. Cut out both large circles and their centers, Fig. g.
8. Punch five equally spaced holes around the edge of both circles with a paper punch, Fig. g.
9. Cut paper large enough to wrap around a deep cardboard box plus a little extra. Tape in place, Fig. h.
10. Cut paper to fit on the unwrapped sides of the box. Tape in place, Fig. i.
11. Trace the end of the tube on the center of one wide side of the wrapped box, Fig. j.
*12. Cut out the traced circle with a scissors, Fig. k. Also make five equally spaced holes around this circle by twisting a sharp pencil into the box.
13. To form the tower, push the tube into the hole on the box. Slip the circles over the tube equally from each other, Fig. l. A piece of tape will keep them from slipping. Push the straw ends of the flowers into the punched holes.

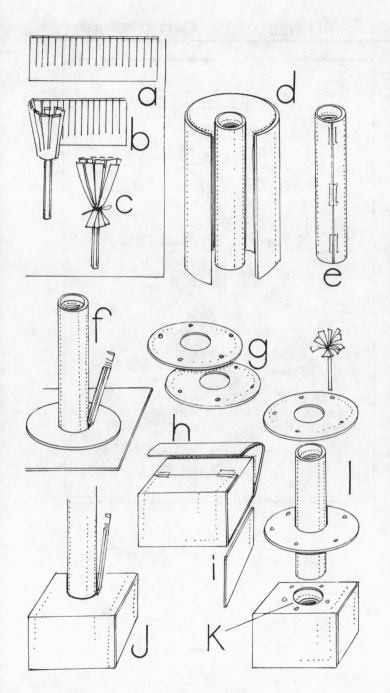

a

b

c

d

e

f

g

h

i

J

K

l

Drauma Doll Favors

A drauma came to old Japan,
Ten years he did stay,
All this prophet did was think,
And then he went away.

THINGS YOU NEED—colored paper, paper cups, tape, scissors, crayons or markers, glue, pencil, candies

1. Wrap a piece of colored paper around a paper cup, Fig. a. Tape in place, Fig. b.
2. Trim away the extra paper around the top and bottom of the cup.
3. Cut a head and flower shapes, similar to the ones shown in the drawing, from colored paper.
4. Draw a face on the head with a crayon or marker.
5. Glue the flower design under the head.
6. Place the open rim of the cup on paper and trace around it with a pencil, Fig. c. Cut out circle.
7. Fill the cup with candies.
8. Squeeze glue around the edge of the circle, Fig. d. Press it against the open end of the cup. Let dry.

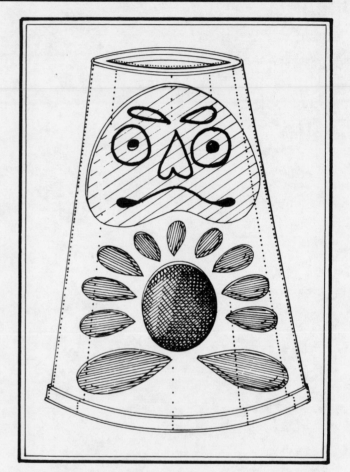

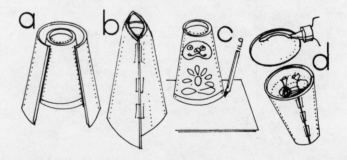

Japanese Breeze Fans

Make some pretty folded fans,
Each friend they're sure to please,
They'll keep the guests so nice and cool –
They're very Japanese!

THINGS YOU NEED—scissors, colored paper, paper punch, cord or yarn

1. Cut colored paper as high as you wish the fan to be and very long.
2. Fold the paper evenly back and forth, until all of the paper is used up, Fig. a.
3. Unfold the paper. Punch a hole into the center of each folded section near one edge with a paper punch, Fig. b.
4. Cut a long piece of cord or yarn. Push one end of the yarn through all holes, Fig. c.
5. Pull the cord or yarn so that the extending ends are the same length, Fig. d.
6. Tie the ends into a tight knot and then a bow.

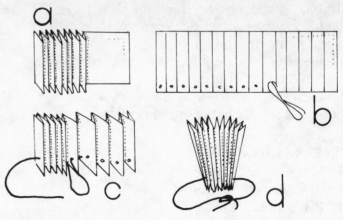

Three Traditional Dolls

We're Hina, Puppet, and Kokeshi,
Dolls with birthday cheer,
We'll bring you joy and happiness
Throughout the coming year.

THINGS YOU NEED—scissors, colored paper, crayons or markers, glue, toothpicks, cardboard bathroom tissue tube, poster paints, brush, pencil, plastic drinking straw, colored and white tissue paper, Ping-Pong ball, yarn, gum ball

A. Hina Doll

1. Cut two small paper circles from colored paper for the head. Draw a face on one with a crayon or marker.
2. Glue the two circles together with one end of a toothpick between them, Fig. a.
3. Fold a square piece of colored paper in half for a blouse. Cut a small V in the center of the fold, Fig. b.
4. Fold a second very long piece of paper in half along the shorter side for a skirt.
5. Slip the toothpick through the V of the blouse. Push the toothpick into the center of the fold of the skirt, Fig. c.
6. Decorate the front of the skirt with paper cut-outs, similar to the ones in the drawing.

B. Kokeshi Doll

1. Make a head using a gumball following steps 7 through 10, doll C.
2. Place the twisted end of the wrapped ball over the top edge of a paper rectangle near one corner, Fig. d.
3. Roll the paper tightly around itself, locking in the twisted tissue.
4. Squeeze glue along the edge of the paper, Fig. e. Press it to the roll, Fig. f.
5. Paint a design on the front of the doll.

C. Puppet Doll

1. Paint a cardboard bathroom tissue tube with poster paint.
2. Make two holes, one opposite the other, near one end of the tube with a sharp pencil, using a twisting motion, Fig. a.
3. Push a plastic drinking straw into the holes for arms, Fig. b.
4. Cut a piece of colored tissue paper a little higher than the tube and long enough to wrap around it plus a little extra.
5. Wrap the paper around the tube a little more than halfway up from the bottom, Fig. c. Tape in place.
6. Fold back the extending paper at the bottom of the tube, Fig. d. The tube should stand.
7. Cut several squares of white tissue paper large enough to wrap around a Ping-Pong ball plus a little extra; see Fig. a, doll B.
8. Place a Ping-Pong ball in the center of the stacked tissue. Bring the sides of the tissue up over the ball and twist them together; see Figs. b and c, doll B.
9. Draw hair and a face on the wrapped ball with a marker.
10. Glue the ball head to the tube with the ends of the tissue tucked inside. Glue a piece of yarn around the waist for a belt, Fig. e.

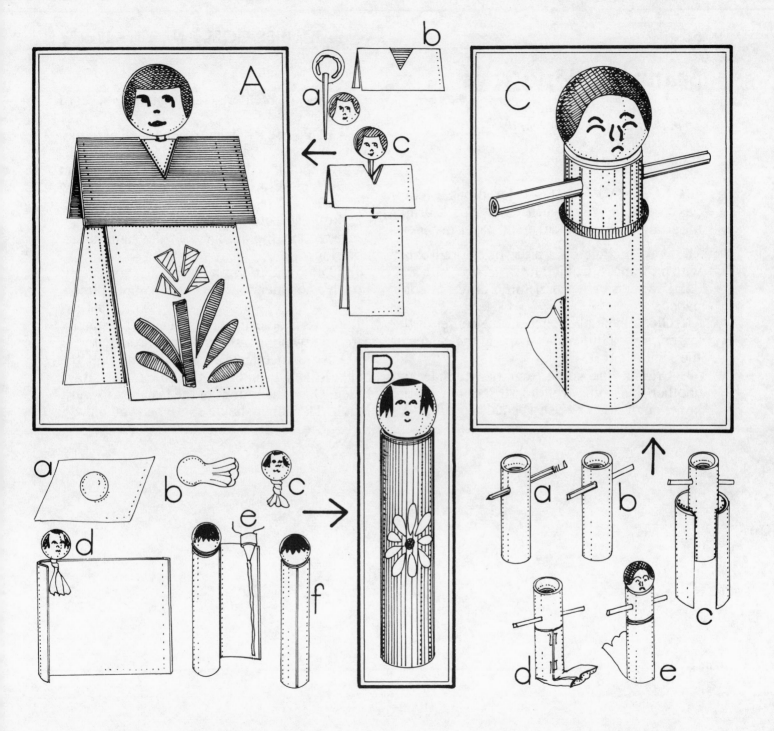

Spinning Wind Toys

Blow gently on this pinwheel,
To make the blades go 'round,
Then listen very closely,
It spins without a sound.

THINGS YOU NEED—colored paper, compass, scissors, glue, pencil, ruler, plastic drinking straws, paper punch, metal paper fasteners

1. Draw a circle on a piece of colored paper with a compass. Cut it out.
2. Draw a smaller circle on a different color paper.
3. Glue the smaller circle in the center of the larger circle. Glue a star shape in the center of the smaller circle, Fig. a.
4. Draw a line going from side to side and another line going from top to bottom on the larger circle, Fig. b. Use a pencil and ruler.

5. Draw lines centered between the first set of lines, Fig. c.
6. Cut along each line up to the smaller circle. Make a small cut along the circle's edge, halfway to the next line, see the heavy lines in Fig. d. A close-up is shown in the square below Fig. d.
7. Roll each cut section around your finger. Each section should curve in the same direction, Fig. e.
8. Flatten the top of a plastic drinking straw. Punch a hole near one end with a paper punch, Fig. f.
9. Make a hole in the center of the star by carefully twisting a sharp pencil through it.
10. Push a metal paper fastener through the hole of the star and into the hole of the straw, Fig. g. Open the prongs of the fastener, loosely, Fig. h. The paper should spin when you blow.

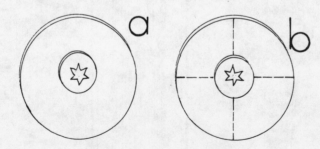

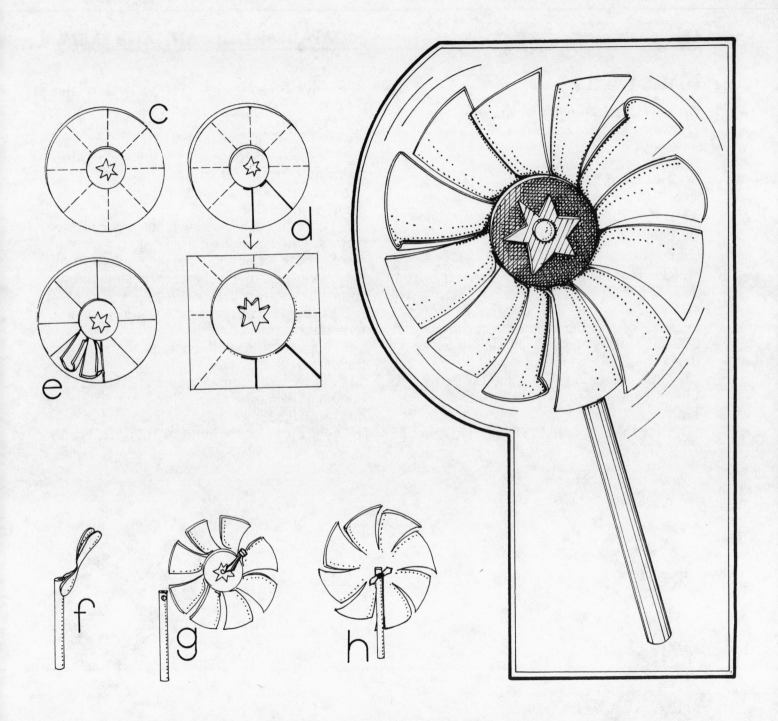

House Kite

To help make your party complete,
This house kite just cannot be beat,
A crepe paper tail,
Will help the kite sail.
It's a wonderful Japanese treat.

THINGS YOU NEED—scissors, heavy cardboard, pencil, ruler, glue, kite string, tissue paper

*1. Cut four small strips the same size from heavy cardboard for the chimney. Use a pencil and a ruler to measure. Cut four more strips twice as long as the first strips for the house. Cut three strips one and one-half times larger than the second strips for the roof.

2. Glue the chimney and house strips into squares, and glue the roof strips into a triangle, Fig. a.

3. Glue the roof onto the house, close to one side. Glue the chimney onto the peak of the roof; study Fig. b.

4. Cut a strip of heavy cardboard that is long enough to extend from the top of the chimney to the bottom of the house. Glue this strip to the frame for a brace, Fig. c.

5. Place the kite on the table with the brace facing you.

6. Tie an end of kite string to the brace where it crosses the top of the house, Fig. d.

7. Squeeze a thin line of glue on all strips of the frame, Fig. d. The brace strip should face you with the string behind it.

8. Lay a piece of tissue paper over the glued frame. Press flat.

9. Cut away the overlapping paper from the frame, Fig. e.

10. Cut a piece of tissue paper as wide as the bottom of the house plus a little extra. Cut slits into one edge for a fringed tail.

11. Glue the tail to the bottom of the kite, Fig. f.

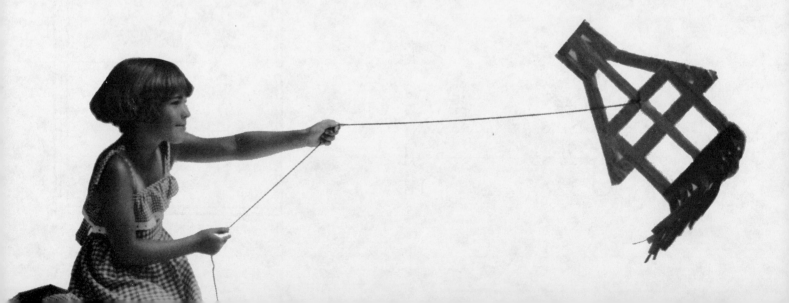

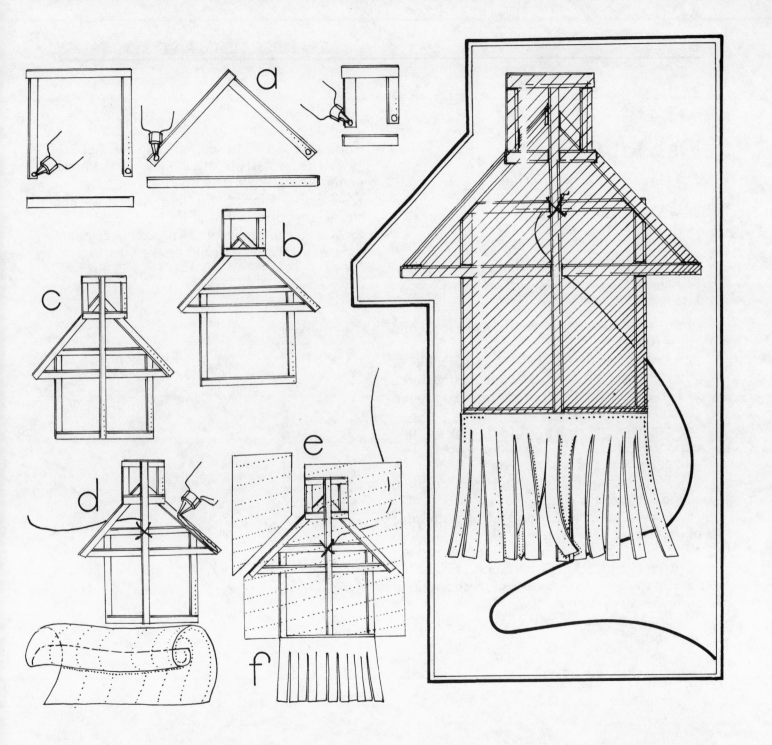

a

b

c

d

e

f

Fish Kite

Kites are made this special day,
And sent aloft and flying.
Tie a string upon this fish,
It wasn't made for frying!

THINGS YOU NEED—scissors, crepe paper, pencil, glue, crayons or markers, heavy wire, kite string.

1. Cut two large rectangles the same size from crepe paper.
2. Draw a fish design on one rectangle, Fig. a.
3. Cut out the fish, as shown in the light area in Fig. a. Use the fish as a pattern to cut out a second fish.
4. Squeeze glue along both side edges of one paper fish shape, Fig. b. Do not squeeze glue along the head and tail.
5. Place the second fish shape over the glued shape. Line up the edges.
6. Draw an eye, scales, and tail on both sides of the fish with a crayon or marker, Fig. c.
*7. Make a circle from heavy wire large enough to fit snugly inside the fish's mouth, Fig. d.
*8. Fit the wire into the fish's mouth a little in from the edges, Fig. e.
9. Squeeze glue along the inside edge of the wire, Fig. f.
10. Fold the edge of the paper over the wire onto the glue and press, Fig. g. It will be easier

if you glue and fold a section at a time. Let dry.
11. Make four evenly spaced holes in the paper under the wire with a sharp pencil.
12. Tie the ends of two short pieces of kite string into opposite holes, Fig. h.
13. Tie an end of the kite string to the center of the two overlapping strings on the kite, Fig. i.

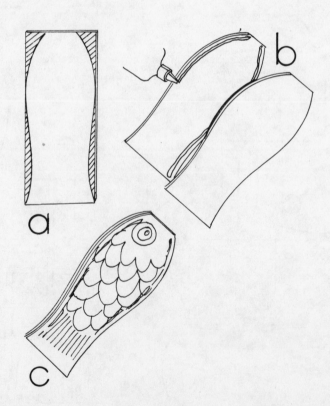

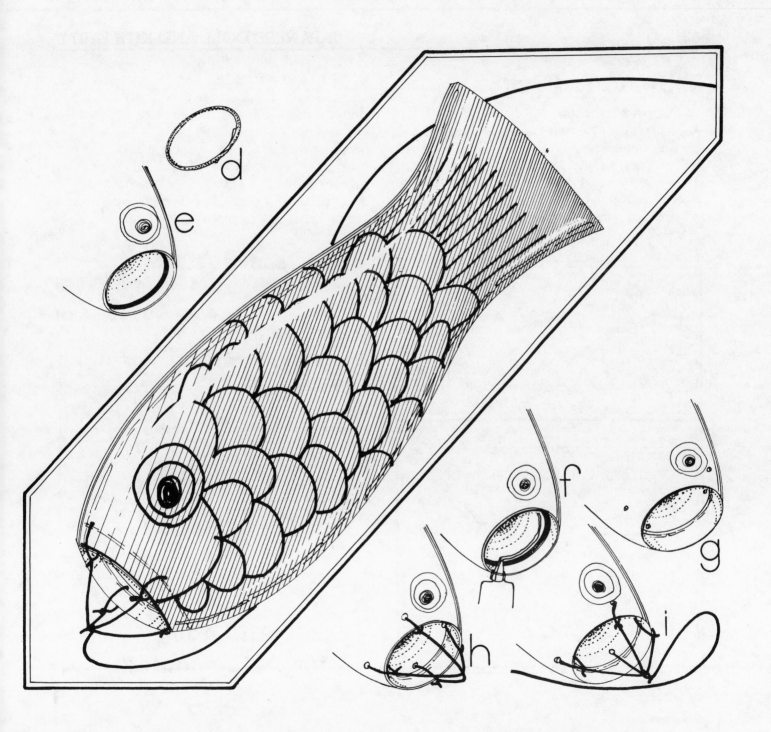

Little Added Extras

A. Kishea Tassels
1. Each guest can wear tassels in his or her hair.
2. Cut small squares of tissue paper. Cut slits halfway across each.
3. Wrap the uncut side of the squares around one end of a plastic drinking straw. Tape in place. Use bobby pins to keep these tassels in place.

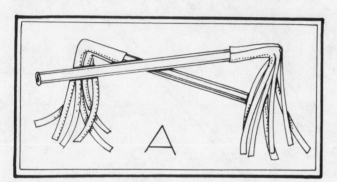

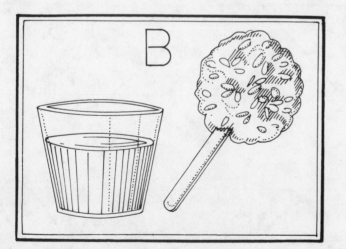

B. Mint Sake and Rice Pops
1. Sake is a Japanese rice wine. To make a pretend mint sake pour chocolate milk into a cup and add peppermint extract.
2. For rice pops melt chocolate bits in a pot over a very low flame. Mix puffed rice cereal into the melted chocolate until well coated.
3. Drop spoonfuls of chocolate puffs on waxed paper. Push an ice cream stick into each spoon-

C. Karate Belts
1. Cut the crepe paper across the short side, creating many strips.
2. Unwind the strips and give one to each guest to wear around his or her waist.

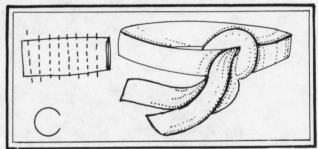

And don't forget the confetti!

Mexican Piñata Party

The nine days before Christmas are a very exciting time for the children of Mexico. There are good things to eat as well as guitar music and dancing. The families act out the story of the first Christmas and at the end of each day there is the breaking of a piñata.

A piñata is a large pottery jar filled with sweets, nuts, fruits, and toys. Children sit in a circle. One at a time each stands and is blindfolded and given several chances to swing at a piñata with a stick. The piñata is on a string, which an adult moves up and down. It is very difficult hitting something you can't see and when the lucky child breaks the jar, everyone scrambles for the falling goodies.

It doesn't have to be Christmas to have a piñata party. A birthday is a perfect occasion. Fill your party room with colorful paper flowers and flags. Make maracas to provide the beat for the Mexican Hat Dance. The highlight of the party will be breaking the paper piñata. When the shower of goodies starts to fall, be sure to shout, "Olé!"

Serape Place Mats

These pretty place mats,
Just wait and you'll see,
Will make your table
As nice as can be.

THINGS YOU NEED—Large sheets of colored paper, crayons or markers

1. Draw a serape design, similar to the one shown in the drawing, on both short ends of a large sheet of colored paper with a crayon or marker.

Serape Invitations

Serape invitations
Say your party's on the way,
These pretty little note cards
Announce the time and day.

THINGS YOU NEED—scissors, colored paper, crayons or markers.

1. Cut a very long colored paper rectangle and fold it in half along the shorter side.
2. Draw a serape design, similar to the one in the drawing, with a crayon or marker.
3. Write the words, "Come to a Piñata Party," on the front of the invitation. Write the party information on the inside.

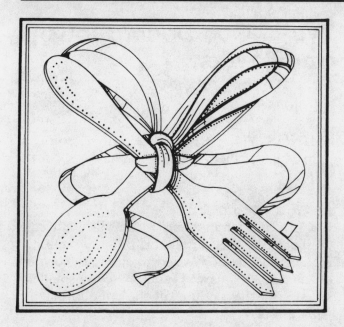

Sol Cake

A sol cake adds more sunshine
To your party mood.
"Sol" means "sun" in Spanish,
And it brightens up the food.

THINGS YOU NEED—cake mix, round cake pan, plate, pink frosting mix, plastic knife, gel icing in a tube

*1. Bake a cake in a round pan. Follow package directions. Remove from the pan and let cool.
2. Mix the frosting, following package directions, and spread it on with a plastic knife.
3. Make a sun design, similar to the one shown in the drawing, with gel icing in a tube.

Ribboned Table Setting

Spoons and forks should all be dressed,
To make your table look its best.

THINGS YOU NEED—plastic spoons and forks, ribbon

1. Cross a plastic fork and spoon.
2. Study the drawing and tie the two together, where they cross, in a criss-cross pattern, with a length of ribbon. Make a bow.

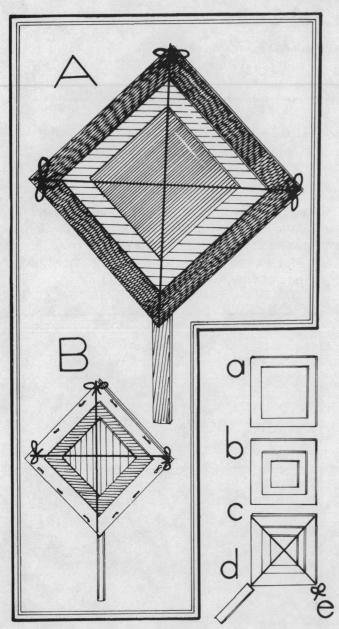

Eye-of-God Decorations and Favors

Candy treats in many flavors
Are inside these pretty favors.

THINGS YOU NEED—scissors, colored paper, glue, ruler, crayons or markers, yarn, stapler, plastic drinking straws, candies

A. Wall Decorations

1. Cut three large squares from different colored papers. They should be different sizes.
2. Glue the medium-sized square in the center of the largest square, Fig. a. Glue the smallest square in the center of the medium-sized square, Fig. b.
3. Draw a line going from corner to corner with a marker and ruler, Fig. c.
4. Glue a brown paper strip to the back of one corner, Fig. d.
5. Staple a yarn bow in the remaining corners on the front, Fig. e.

B. Fan Favors

1. Make two small eyes-of-god as above without the brown paper strip.
2. Staple the two together with candies between them. Staple a plastic drinking straw at one corner.

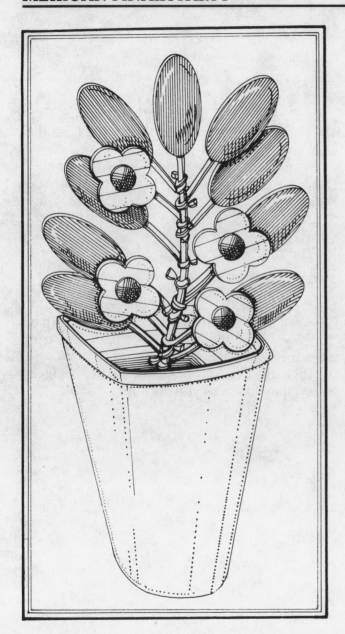

Pot of Flowers Favors

Mexican in flavor,
Colorful and gay,
Pretty pots of flowers
Add sunshine to the day.

THINGS YOU NEED — scissors, pipe cleaners, colored paper, glue, paper cups, candy

1. Cut pipe cleaners into short pieces.
2. Cut oval-shaped leaves from green paper.
3. Glue a leaf to one end of the short pipe cleaner stems, Fig. a. Make several.
4. Glue a leaf to an uncut pipe cleaner.
5. Twist the small stems around the uncut pipe cleaner, Fig. b.
6. Cut a flower shape and glue it to the end of short pipe cleaner stems, Fig. c. Make several.
7. Twist the flower stems around the uncut pipe cleaner, between the leaves.
8. Make the opening of a paper cup square by flattening the upper half (open end) together, Fig. d, then opening the cup.
9. Flatten the upper half of the cup in the opposite direction from the first fold, Fig. e. Open the cup. The folds will make the opening square instead of round.
10. Fill the cup with candy. Add the flowers.

Señorita Centerpiece

For your table a cute señorita,
As a centerpiece no one can beat her.
She'll delight every guest,
'Cause she's prettily dressed,
And the name of this doll is Conchita.

THINGS YOU NEED—large sheets of colored paper or poster board (oaktag), tape, pencil, compass, markers, pipe cleaners, glue, colored crepe paper or tissue paper

1. Roll a large sheet of poster board or colored paper into a cone and tape, Fig. a.
2. Trim the bottom edge to form a circle. The cone should stand straight, Fig. b.
3. Draw a ring on a piece of paper with a compass. Draw a smaller ring within that one, Fig. c. Cut out the ring including the piece from the center.
4. Place the ring over the point of the cone. Draw a face under the ring with a marker, Fig. d.
5. Cut narrow crepe paper or tissue paper strips.
6. Cut slits into one long edge of the strips, Fig. e.
7. Tape two pipe cleaners to the cone, below the face, for arms. Glue on paper hands, Fig. f.
8. Wrap the first slit strip around the bottom of the cone. Tape the ends on the back and trim away any extra paper.
9. Tape the remaining strips up to the face, overlapping them as you go, Fig. g.

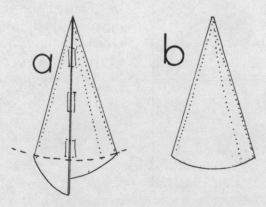

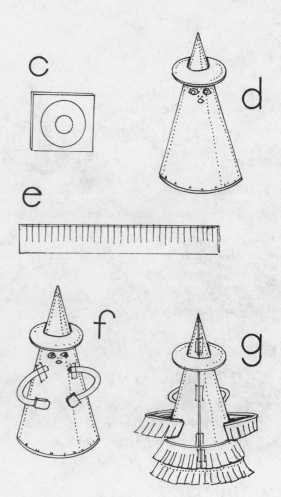

c

d

e

f

g

Fiesta Flags

Lacy flags that gently sway
Make pretty decorations.
Trace the pattern from the book
Or make your own creations.

THINGS YOU NEED—scissors, colored tissue paper, pencil, wire clothes hangers, tape, yarn or cord

1. Cut a piece of tissue paper as wide as a wire clothes hanger and as long as the pattern in the book.
2. Place one end of the tissue over the pattern (with the arrows) and, using a pencil, trace the pattern onto the paper.
3. Fold the paper evenly back and forth with the tracing on top. The folds should be no wider than the pattern, Fig. a. Use up all the paper, Fig. b.
4. Cut out the pattern through all layers of the folded paper, following the drawn lines, Fig. c. Do not cut the lines of the tracing which are shown as dotted lines in the pattern.
5. Open up the cut paper. Fold the top (the straight edge) over a wire coat hanger and tape. For a line of flags, tape several to a long piece of cord or yarn instead of clothes hangers.

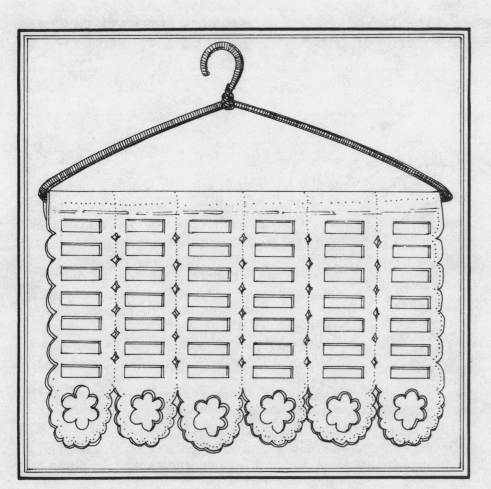

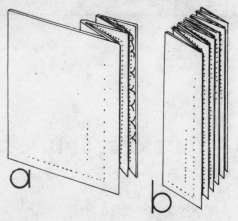

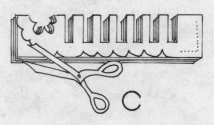

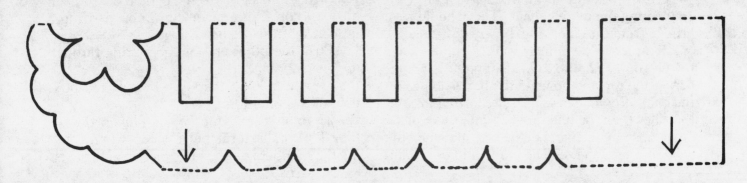

Mission Bell Toss Game

These mission bells are hanging still,
Not a one is ringing,
By using just a little skill,
You can start them swinging.

THINGS YOU NEED—tape, large detergent powder box, crayons or markers, ruler, scissors, poster paint, brush, pencil, plastic drinking straws, colored paper, string, beads, paper clips, bells, Ping-Pong balls.

1. Tape the open end of a large detergent box closed.

2. Draw three sets of parallel lines (close to each other), dividing the front of the box into four sections, Fig. a. Use a ruler.

3. Continue the lines along the sides and the back of the box.

4. Draw lines in the two middle sections (X), connecting the parallel lines. They should be a little in from the sides, Fig. b.

5. Draw two lines going from the parallel lines to the top of the box (Z). Continue the lines across the top and down to the parallel lines on the back, Fig. b. These lines are farther in from the sides than the lines in the middle sections.

*6. Cut away the parts of the box shown by the shaded areas, Fig. c. The parallel lines around the sides of the box remain uncut.

7. Cut out five windows between the parallel lines in the middle sections on one side of the box; shaded areas in Fig. d.

8. Paint the box.

9. Make a hole above each window with a sharp pencil, using a twisting motion. Continue twisting the pencil out through the back of the box, Fig. e.

10. Push a plastic drinking straw through each hole above the windows, and out the back of the box, Fig. f.

11. Roll colored paper into a small cone and tape, Fig. g. Trim edge to form a circle, Fig. h. Make five bells in this way.

12. Write a number on each bell with a marker.

13. Tie a knot in one end of five lengths of string.

14. String a bead on each length and rest each on the knot. Tie a paper clip to each string a little away from the bead, Fig. i.

15. Push the other end of each string through the inside point of the bells.

16. Tie the bells to the straws inside the box, behind the windows.

17. To play the game, each player throws Ping-Pong balls at the bells. Keep score, totaling the numbers on the bells hit by each player.

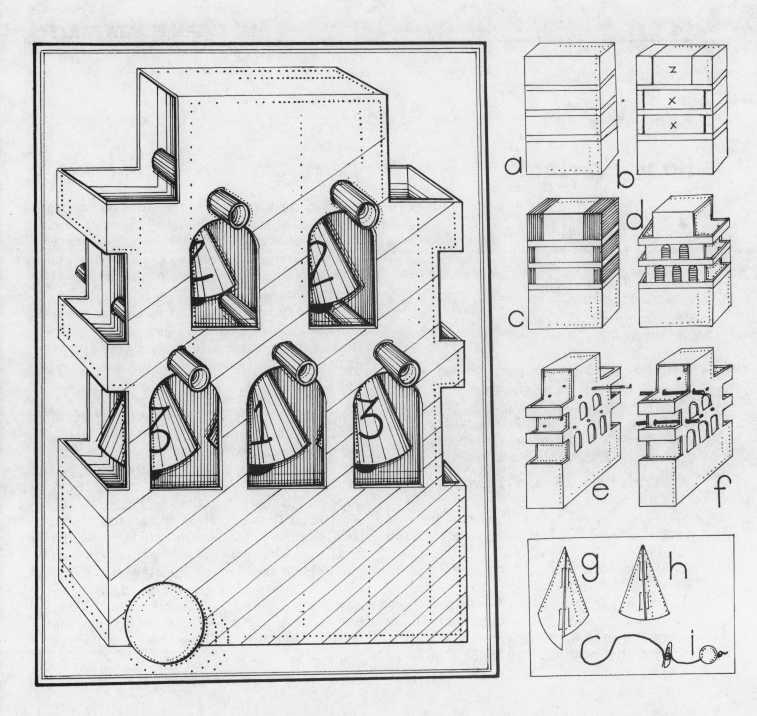

Hanging Piñata

It's a Mexican tradition,
As all the children know,
To hang a filled piñata
And sway it to and fro.

Then all the little children,
Blindfolded try to break
the piñata packed full with toys
and sweets for all to take.

THINGS YOU NEED—large brown paper bag, small toys and wrapped candies, heavy cord, sewing thread, newspaper, white glue, paper cup, waxed paper, brush, poster paint, colored paper, tape, scissors, crepe paper or tissue paper, broom, blindfold.

1. Fill a large brown paper bag with small toys and candies, Fig. a.
2. Gather the open end of the bag. Tie a long piece of heavy cord tightly around the gathered end, Fig. b.
3. Wrap sewing thread around the bag in every direction to give it added strength, Fig. c.
4. Tear newspaper into strips.
5. Pour glue into a paper cup. Dilute it by mixing in a bit of water.
6. Place the newspaper strips on a sheet of waxed paper. Brush one side of the strips with glue.
7. Lay the glued side of the strips on the bag covering the thread completely, up to the tie, Fig. d. Let dry overnight. (If you are in a hurry, you can eliminate this papier mâché step and just decorate a plain paper bag.)
8. Paint the bag, Fig. e.
9. Make four large cones from colored paper and tape. Trim the bottom edge, Fig. f.
10. Cut five long pieces of colored crepe paper or tissue paper. Cut slits along one long edge, Fig. g.
11. Tape the uncut edge of a slit paper over the point of a cone, Fig. h. Roll the entire length of paper around the point and tape for a tassel. Tape one tassel to each cone.
12. Tape the cones to the sides of the bag, Fig. i.
13. Roll the last slitted paper around itself. Tape it to the bottom of the bag, Fig. j.
14. To play the game, tie the piñata to a broom handle. Have a tall person hold it above the heads of the players. The players are blindfolded and each in turn swings at the piñata with a stick while the piñata is being raised and lowered by the person holding the broom. When the bag breaks, the goodies will fall out, and all the players try to collect as many as they can.

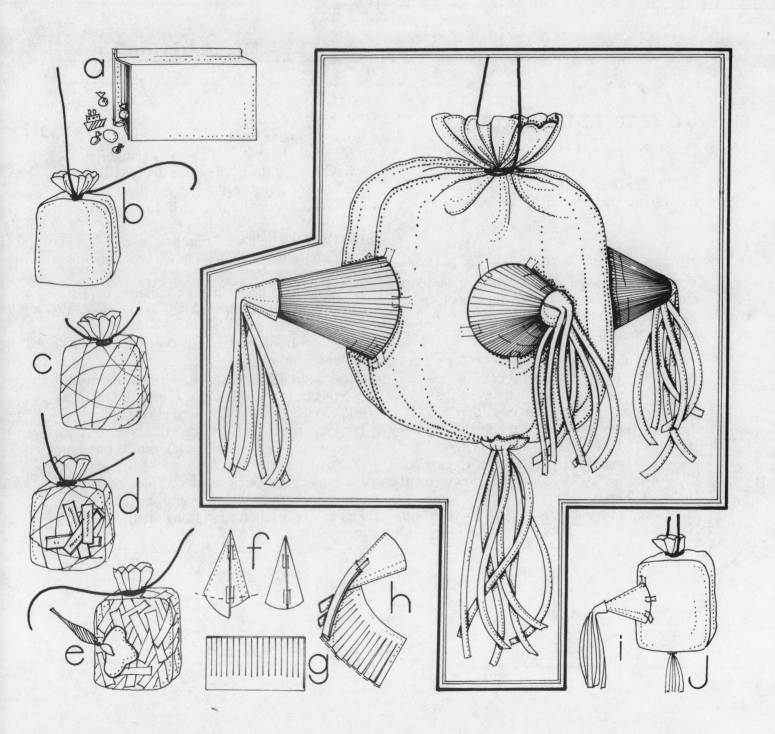

Shaking Maracas

When doing the Mexican Hat Dance,
Maracas will keep you on beat,
Shake them and get yourself moving,
By tapping real hard with your feet.

THINGS YOU NEED—round balloons, newspaper, waxed paper, white glue, paper cup, brush, scissors, fine sandpaper, poster paint, brush, crayons or markers, pencil, dried beans, wooden dowels, saw

1. Blow up two round balloons to the size of a grapefruit. Knot the necks, Fig. a.
2. Tear newspaper into narrow strips. Place the strips on a sheet of waxed paper.
3. Pour glue into a paper cup. Dilute it by mixing in a bit of water.
4. Brush one side of the strips with glue.
5. Layer the strips, glue side down, on the balloons, Fig. b.
6. Cover both balloons completely with about three layers of glued strips. Smooth the last layer with your hands.
7. Allow the balloons to dry overnight.
8. Cut away the necks when dry, Fig. c. Cover the holes with more glued strips. Let dry.
9. Sand the balloons with fine sandpaper, Fig. d.
10. Paint the balloons, Fig. e.
11. Decorate the balloons with a crayon or marker.
12. Make two holes in each balloon, opposite each other, with a sharp pencil, using a twisting motion, Fig. f.
13. Push dried beans into one hole of each balloon, Fig. g.
*14. Ask an adult to saw a wooden dowel into two pieces for handles. The dowel should be as thick as a pencil or slightly thicker.
15. Push the dowels through the holes of each balloon. One end should stick out of one hole slightly.
16. Squeeze a thick layer of glue around the dowels where they enter and exit the holes, Fig. h. Let dry before shaking them.

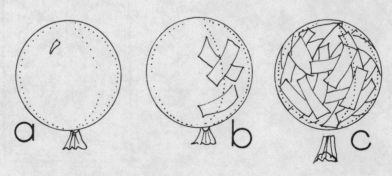

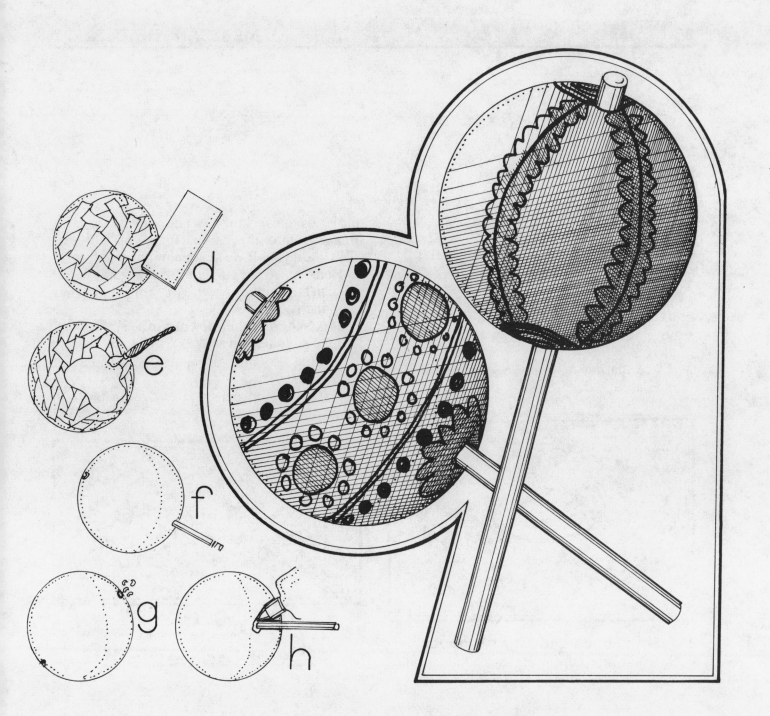

Little Added Extras

A Mexican Hat Dance Mat

1. Cut a very large circle from colored paper.
2. Draw a smaller circle in the center and a wavy line around the edge with a crayon or marker.
3. Place the hat mat on the floor and do fun dances around it.

apple wedges, grapes, cherries, mandarin oranges—into the compartment of ice cube trays. Add your favorite fruit punch and freeze.
2. Remove frozen cubes from refrigerator and place in large punch bowl. Pour citrus juice over the punch cubes.
3. Mix salt and chili powder in a plastic bag. Drop in peanuts and shake.
4. Place a spoonful of peanuts on a square of clear kitchen wrap.
5. Gather the corners and tie with a piece of colored yarn.

B. Piñata Punch and Angry Peanuts

1. Sprinkle tiny cut-up pieces of fruit—pine-

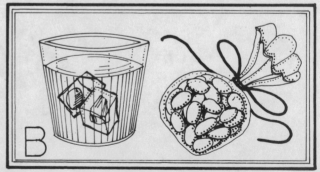

And don't forget the confetti!

American Indian Party

All across America there are many Indian nations each with different costumes and customs. Something they share is the love of games.

Pretend your friends are Indians from many nations. It is your birthday, so why not invite them to a get-together party everyone will remember.

Greet each guest with a feathered headband. Prepare games for them to play and when the competition is over, give each winner a special Indian medallion. Then it will be time to gather around the table to feast on fine party food.

Arrow Place Mats

The arrow place mats mark the places
Where you'll feed all hungry faces.

THINGS YOU NEED — scissors, large sheets of colored paper, crayons or markers

1. Cut out an arrow from a large sheet of colored paper, similar to the one shown in the drawing.
2. Write the name of a guest on the pointed end with a crayon or marker.

Arrow Invitations

Indian arrows sent to friends say,
"Come to my powwow, it's my special day."

THINGS YOU NEED — colored paper, crayons or markers, scissors

1. Fold a long strip of colored paper in half along the shorter side.
2. Draw an arrow design, with the point at the open end.
3. Cut out the arrow through both layers of folded paper. Do not cut along the fold.
4. Write the words, "THIS WAY TO A PARTY," on the front with a crayon or marker. Write the party information on the inside.

Cupcake Totem Pole

This totem looks scary and tall,
But it frightens no one at all,
Made of icing and cake,
It's easy to bake,
And will quickly be eaten by all.

THINGS YOU NEED—cupcake liners, cupcake tin, cake mix, white frosting mix, plastic knife, gel icing in a tube, tracing paper, pencil, scissors, colored paper, cookie sheet, aluminum foil.

*1. Place cupcake liners inside the compartments of a cupcake tin. Bake one cupcake for each guest. Follow package directions. Remove from the tin and let cool.

2. Mix the frosting according to package directions. Spread evenly on the cupcakes with a plastic knife.

3. Make a face on each cupcake with gel icing.

4. Cut long triangles for wings or small triangles for ears from colored paper for the top cupcakes.

5. Cover a cookie sheet with aluminum foil or colored paper. Arrange the cupcakes in one or two totem poles.

6. Push the paper wings or ears into the frosting of the top cupcake.

Totem Pole Favors

Four little Indians,
Looking fine and dandy,
Wrapped around a cardboard tube,
Filled with party candy.

THINGS YOU NEED—scissors, colored paper or tissue paper, cardboard bathroom tissue tubes, crayons or markers, candies, tape, ribbon or yarn

1. Cut a piece of colored paper or tissue paper wide enough to wrap around a cardboard bathroom tissue tube. It should be twice as high as the tube.
2. Place the cardboard tube in the center of the paper. Mark on the paper where the ends of the tube fall, Fig. a.
3. Draw lines across the shorter side of the paper with a crayon or marker at the marks. Draw three more lines equally spaced between the first lines, Fig. b.
4. Draw a face in the center of each of the four areas between the lines, Fig. c.
5. Fill the tube with candies.
6. Place the tube in the center of the paper. Be sure the faces are facing the table, Fig. d.
7. Roll the paper around the tube and tape in place, Fig. e.
8. Cut slits into both ends of the rolled paper up to the tube, Fig. f.
9. Tie both ends of the rolled favor with ribbon or yarn, Fig. g.

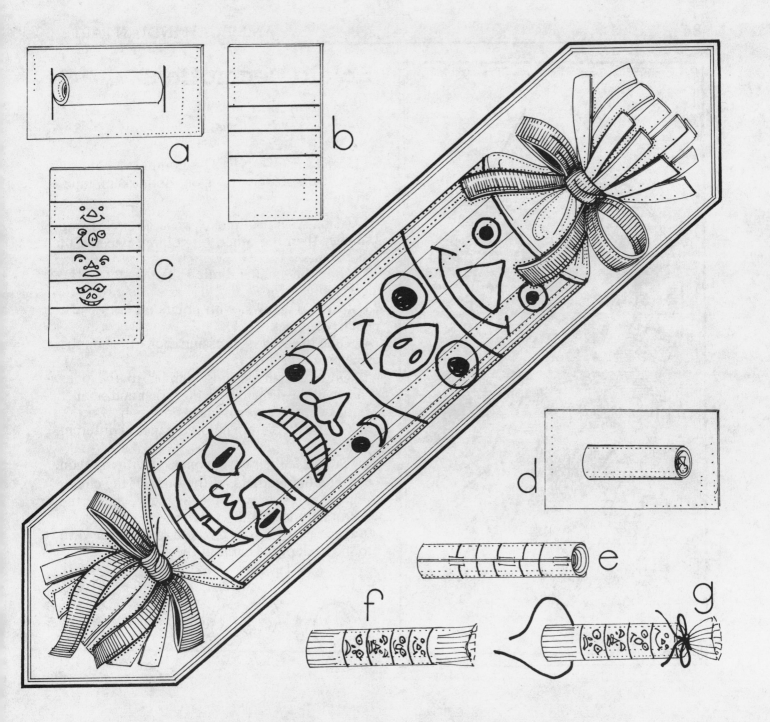

a

b

c

d

e

f

g

Shield Decorations

Hang this decoration.
One for every Indian nation.

THINGS YOU NEED — compass, colored paper, scissors, glue, crayons or markers, tape, string.

1. Using a compass, make two large circles, one smaller than the other, on colored paper. Cut them out.
2. Glue the smaller circle in the center of the larger circle, Fig. a.
3. Cut two arrows, with points on both ends, from red paper.
4. Glue the arrows, crossing each other, on the smaller circle, Fig. b.
5. Draw Indian designs, similar to the ones shown in the drawing, on the larger and smaller circles with a crayon or marker, Fig. b.
6. Cut feathers from colored paper in different sizes.
7. Draw a feather design on each with a crayon.
8. Tape the feathers on the back of the circle, Fig. c. The side with the feathers will be the bottom of the shield.
9. Tape both ends of a length of string or yarn to the back of the circle at the sides, Fig. d.

Tall
Totem Pole

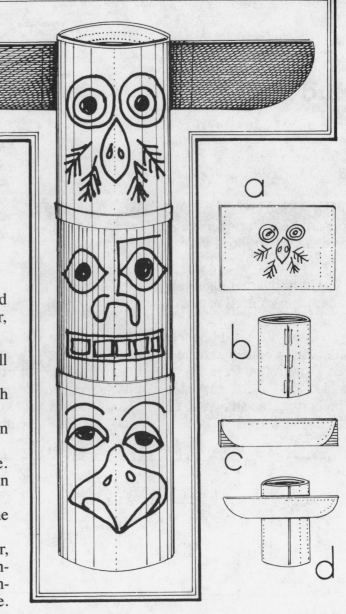

An Indian carved a totem
From a tree that stood so tall,
And placed it standing in a hole,
So it would never fall.

The totem stayed for many years
Beside his cabin door,
And kept the evil spirits far,
They bothered him no more.

THINGS YOU NEED — scissors, poster board (oaktag), crayons or markers, colored paper, glue, masking tape.

1. Cut several long poster board rectangles, all the same size.
2. Draw a bird or animal in the center of each rectangle with crayons or markers, Fig. a.
3. Roll the rectangles into cylinders. Tape in place, Fig. b.
4. Cut a long, narrow colored paper rectangle. Round each short end; see shaded area in Fig. c.
5. Glue or tape the cut paper to the back of one cylinder for wings, Fig. d.
6. Tape the cylinders one on top of the other, with the winged face on top. Tape several cylinder heads on top of one another for a centerpiece or at least six for a standing totem pole.

Bird Masks

Design some Indian bird masks
For all the braves and squaws.
Make each one look real scary
By adding beaks and claws.

THINGS YOU NEED — scissors, colored paper, pencil, paper punch, loose-leaf reinforcements, ribbon, yarn or string, crayons or markers

1. Cut large rectangles about as wide as your face, from colored paper. Fold in half along the longer side.
2. Draw a curved line from the top corner to the bottom corner at the open end, Fig. a.
3. Draw a line from the bottom corner on the folded side to the curved line, a little up from the bottom, as shown in Fig. b. Cut out along the drawn lines.

4. Draw a nose in the center on the folded side. Cut along the lines of the nose; see dotted line in Fig. b. Do not cut the nose off the mask.
5. Open the folded paper. Place it over your face and mark with a pencil where your eyes fall.
6. Cut out a circle around each pencil mark, Fig. c.
7. Punch a hole on opposite sides of the mask with a paper punch, Fig. d.
8. Glue a loose-leaf reinforcement over each hole to prevent the paper from tearing. Knot a length of ribbon, yarn, or string into each hole, Fig. e.
9. Decorate the mask with colored paper cut-outs or draw designs with a crayon or marker.
10. Pull out the cut nose when you wear the mask, Fig. f.

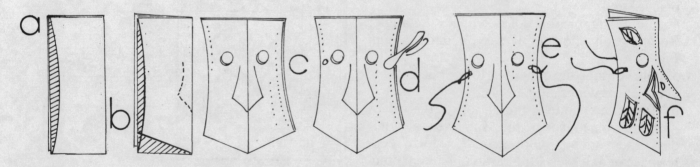

Feathered Headband

Make many Indian headbands
For all your friends to wear,
Be sure each gets a feather
Then tie them 'round their hair.

THINGS YOU NEED—scissors, colored paper, plastic drinking straws, white glue, crayons or markers, felt (optional), paper punch, loose-leaf reinforcements, cord or yarn

1. Cut two colored paper rectangles the size you wish the feather to be.
2. Place a straw on the center of one rectangle. One end of the straw should extend slightly below the paper, Fig. a.
3. Squeeze a thin, wavy line of glue on both sides of the straw, Fig. a.
4. Place the other rectangle over the glued rectangle. Line up the edges, Fig. b. Let dry.
5. Draw a feather shape on the paper, Fig. c.
6. Cut out the feather. Draw a design on each feather, similar to the one shown in the drawing, with a crayon or marker, Fig. d.
7. Cut a long strip from colored paper, or, better still, from felt. It should be long enough to wrap about three-quarters around the head.
8. Punch a hole into both ends of the paper or felt with a paper punch, Fig. e.
9. Glue a loose-leaf reinforcement over each hole to prevent the paper from tearing. Knot a length of yarn or string in each hole, Fig. f.
10. Draw Indian designs on the band with a crayon or marker.
11. Tape the feather in the center of the band.

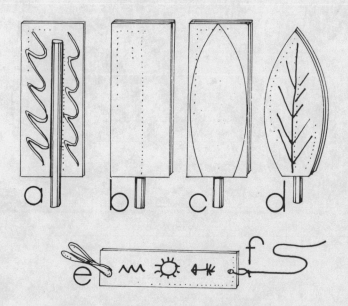

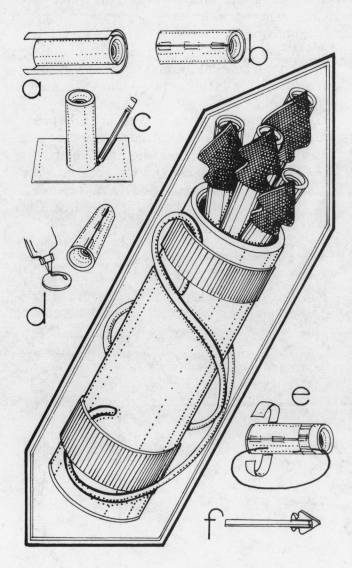

Quiver and Arrows

Make arrows and a quiver
For every party guest.
Indians used to hunt with them
In the Wild Wild West.

THINGS YOU NEED — scissors, colored paper, cardboard bathroom tissue tube or paper towel tube, tape, pencil, glue, cord or yarn, plastic drinking straws

1. Cut a piece of paper as high as a bathroom tissue or paper towel tube, whichever size you choose, and long enough to wrap around it plus a little extra, Fig. a.
2. Wrap the paper around the tube and tape in place, Fig. b.
3. Place the end of the tube on a piece of lightweight cardboard and trace around the end with a pencil, Fig. c.
4. Cut out the traced circle.
5. Squeeze glue around the edge of the circle, Fig. d.
6. Press the circle on one end of the tube. Let dry.
7. Attach one end of a long piece of cord or yarn to one end of the tube with a long piece of tape, Fig. e. Repeat with the other end of the cord at the other end of the tube.
8. Cut out colored paper arrowheads. Glue or tape them to one end of several plastic drinking straws, Fig. f. Make many arrows.
9. Place the arrows inside the quiver and wear it around your neck.

Indian Competition

*An Indian competition
With all guests joining in,
They'll have fun at these four games
And each will try to win.*

THINGS YOU NEED — paper, scissors, paper punch, yarn, glue, cardboard, sponge, dried beans, plastic knife, marker, popping corn, tin can, small stones, toothpicks

Canoe Race

1. Fold a piece of paper in half. It should be twice as long as it is high.
2. Cut a curve into both ends of the paper, starting at the corners of the open end down to the folded edge; see shaded area in Fig. a.
3. Punch holes through both layers of paper along the open end and down both sides with a paper punch, Fig. b.
4. Push one end of two long pieces of yarn or cord through the bottom hole in the lower left-hand corner of both layers; see arrow in Fig. c. Tie tightly.
5. Weave the two yarns at the same time through the holes at the end of the canoe. Also weave both yarns through two holes at the top, Fig. c.
6. Separate the yarns. Weave each piece through the holes of the top edge, stopping one or two holes from the opposite end, Fig. d.
7. Weave the two lengths together into the remaining holes at the top and down the end.
8. Tie the ends of the yarns together. Cut

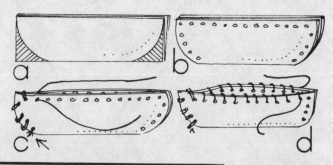

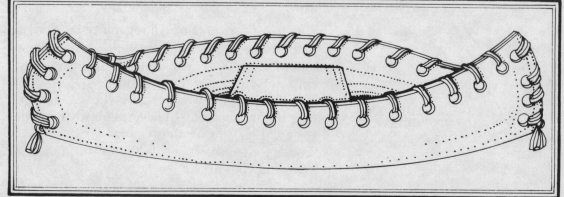

away the extra yarn.

9. Glue a small piece of cardboard or sponge inside the canoe to keep the sides pushed out and the bottom flat, see Fig. e.

10. Make several canoes. To play the game, place the canoes at a starting line. The players have to blow their canoes across a determined distance to a finish line without using their hands. First one over wins.

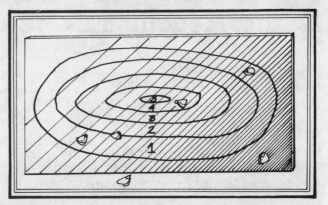

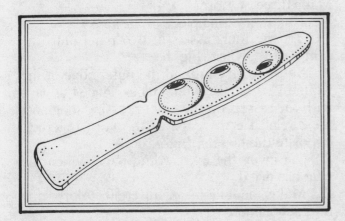

ping corn and tosses them onto the paper. Add up the numbers in the rings where the kernels landed. The player with the highest score wins.

Bean Race

1. Place three dried beans on a plastic knife.
2. Each player holds the handle of a knife in his or her hand.
3. The players run to a finish line, trying not to drop any beans.

Corn Toss

1. Draw several circles within circles on a large piece of paper with a marker.
2. Write a number in each ring.
3. To play, each player gets five kernels of pop-

Sticks and Stones

1. Cover a tin can with paper and decorate it with Indian symbols.
2. Collect five small stones, all the same size. Write a number from one to five on each stone.
3. To play, each player stands several feet away and tries in turn to toss the stones into the can. Add up the number on the stones that each player has tossed in the can. Record each score on the floor with toothpicks. High-score wins.

Warrior Medallion

The winner of each party game,
Proud as a mighty stallion,
Gets to wear around her neck,
An Indian warrior's medallion.

THINGS YOU NEED — glue, paper cup, brush, white paper, yarn, scissors, cardboard, embroidery thread or string, colored paper

1. Pour a little glue into a paper cup.
2. Paint a thick large circle of glue on a sheet of white paper with a brush, Fig. a.
3. Wind yarn around itself on the glue, starting at the center of the circle, Fig. b. Press the yarn into the glue as you go. Fill in the circle with one colored yarn or change colors as you wind.
4. Cut a cardboard rectangle as high as your hand.
5. Wrap embroidery thread around the cardboard several times, Fig. c.
6. Tie all the thread, at the top of the cardboard, together with a piece of yarn, Fig. d. Cut through the thread at the bottom of the cardboard, Fig. e. Remove the thread from the cardboard.
7. Cut a small strip of colored paper. Wrap it tightly around the top of the tied thread, Fig. f. Glue or tape in place to make a tassel, Fig. g. Make three or more.
8. Cut a very long piece of yarn.
9. Tie the four tassels in two pairs onto the center of the yarn, Fig. h.
10. Squeeze glue around the outer edge of the wound yarn on the white paper. Place the yarn with the tassels on the glue, pressing it against the circle. Tie the ends of the yarn together, opposite the tassels, Fig. i.
11. Cut away the extra white paper when the glue has dried.
12. Make medallions in different colors, one for each game.

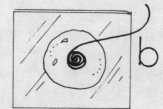

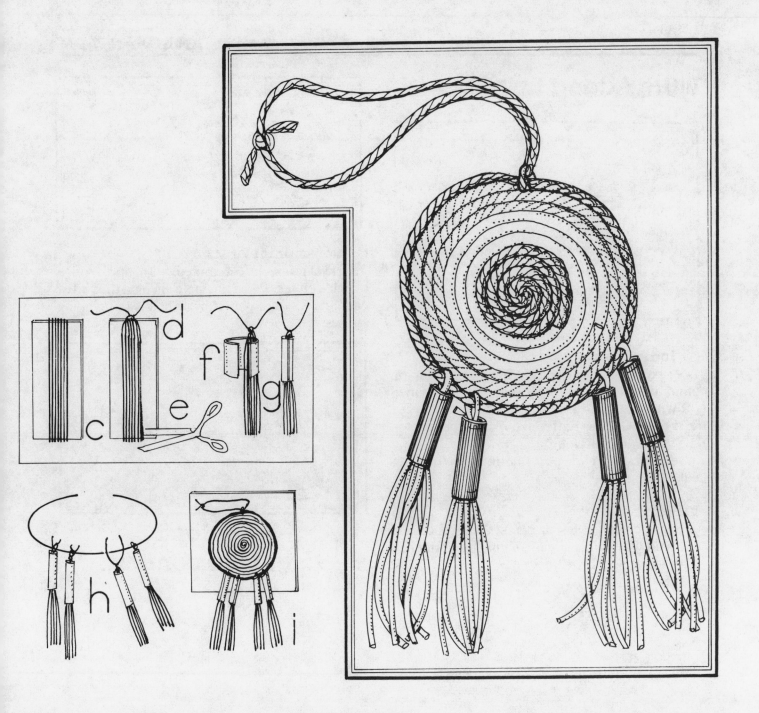

c d e f g h i

Little Added Extras

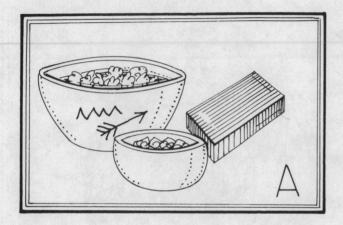

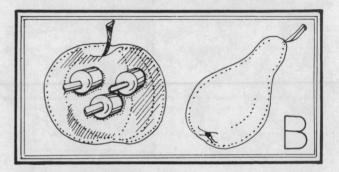

C. Ceremonial Punch

Serve grape juice, mixed with apple juice over ice cubes. Place an apple slice on the rim of each glass. Tape paper arrowheads to drinking straws.

A. Indian Snacks

1. Make Indian bowls by drawing symbols on china bowls with markers that can be washed off with water, or use disposable bowls.
2. Fill bowls with buttered popcorn, peanuts in the shell, and corn chips.
3. Serve ice cream pops along with the cupcakes.

B. Harvest Fruit

Serve crisp apples or pears. Make faces on the fruit with miniature marshmallows attached with toothpicks.

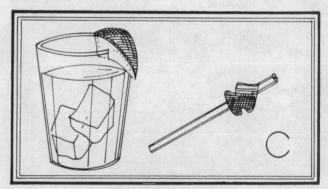

And don't forget the confetti!

Chinese Red Egg Party

If you live in China, your birth is celebrated a month after you are born with a "Red Egg Party." People sit down to a delicious dinner, and the host dyes eggs red for this happy event.

Why not have a red egg birthday party this year. Red is the color for luck, so as a sign of friendship, give each guest a red egg.

Make your Chinese party a colorful occasion. Lanterns and fiery dragons are the traditional decorations. Noisemakers, hats, and a cupcake dragon add to the atmosphere.

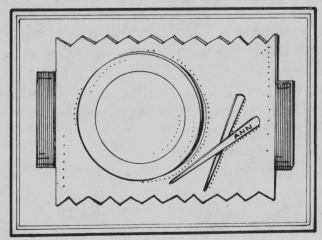

Birthday Party," on the outside of the card with a crayon or marker. Color the top and bottom parts of the lantern a different shade. Write the party information on the inside.

Lantern Invitations

Send a message warm and hearty,
To announce your Chinese party.

THINGS YOU NEED — pencil, colored paper, scissors, crayons or markers

1. Fold a long piece of paper in half across the shorter side.
2. Draw a lantern design on the front similar to the one shown in the small drawing.
3. Cut out the lantern through both layers of the paper. Do not cut along the folded edge.
4. Write the words, "Come to a Red Egg

Lantern Place Mats

Off lantern mats each guest will eat
On food so good – a party treat.

THINGS YOU NEED — pencil, colored paper, scissors, glue, crayons or markers

1. Draw and cut out a lantern shape from white paper, similar to the one shown in the drawing.
2. Cut two dark colored rectangles, one for each end of the lantern. Glue in place.
3. Cut a pair of paper chopsticks from colored paper. Chopsticks look like jumbo toothpicks. Write the name of a guest on one of the chopsticks with a crayon or marker.

Chinese Hats

Upon each head, round or flat,
Place a sloping Chinese hat.

THINGS YOU NEED—large sheets of colored paper, tape, scissors, stapler, ribbon

1. Roll a large sheet of colored paper into a wide cone. Tape in place, Fig. a.
2. Trim the bottom edge to form a circle, Fig. b.
3. Staple two lengths of ribbon, one opposite the other, on the inside of the hat.

Red Egg Souvenir

Red eggs are pretty and taste good too,
Be sure each guest gets one from you.

THINGS YOU NEED—hard-boiled eggs, white crayon, red food coloring or red egg dye, metal tablespoon, paper towels

1. Write the name of a guest on a dry, unshelled egg with a white crayon.
2. Mix food coloring in a cup of water. If you use egg dye, follow package directions. Place the egg on a metal tablespoon and dip it into the dye mixture for a few minutes.
3. Remove the egg from the cup and dry on a paper towel.

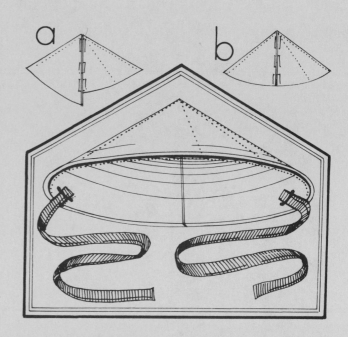

Slinky Cupcake Dragon

This dragon so fiery and vicious,
Isn't really considered malicious,
'Cause his roar is a fake,
He's just made of cake,
Which everyone finds quite delicious.

THINGS YOU NEED—cupcake liners, cupcake tin, cake mix, white frosting mix, plastic knife, cookie sheet, aluminum foil, gel icing in a tube, tracing paper, pencil, scissors, red paper

*1. Place cupcake liners inside the compartments of a cupcake tin. Bake one cupcake for each guest. Follow package directions. Remove from the tin and let cool.
2. Mix the frosting according to package directions. Spread evenly on the cupcakes with a plastic knife.
3. Cover a cookie sheet with aluminum foil. Arrange the cupcakes in a snakelike design.
4. Make a dragon face on the first cupcake with gel icing in a tube. Make a squiggly design across the center of each remaining cupcake.
5. Trace the designs from this book on a sheet of tracing paper. Cut out the tracings.
6. Trace around the cut-outs on red paper. Trace two curled horns (1) for the head cupcake, three tails (2) for the last cupcake, and a wing (3) for each cupcake between the head and tail.
7. Cut out the traced patterns. Push them into the frosting on the cupcakes, as shown in the drawing.

Hanging Lantern Decorations

*Make lanterns in different colors
And hang them from the ceiling,
To give your party what it needs —
A festive, Chinese feeling.*

THINGS YOU NEED—scissors, white and colored paper, glue, stapler or tape, paper punch, string

1. Cut two colored paper strips as long as the long side of a sheet of white paper.
2. Glue the strips to the top and bottom edges of the paper, Fig. a.
3. Fold the paper in half, Fig. b.
4. Cut slits into the folded edge of the paper up to the colored strips, Fig. c. The slits should be equally spaced.
5. Open the paper and roll it so the short sides meet, Fig. d. Overlap the ends slightly.
6. Staple or tape the lantern closed at the top and bottom along the colored strips, Fig. e.
7. Punch two holes, one opposite the other, into one colored strip, Fig. f. This will be the top of the lantern.
8. Push the ends of a long piece of string through the holes and make a knot, Fig. f.
9. Make many lanterns and hang them around your party room.

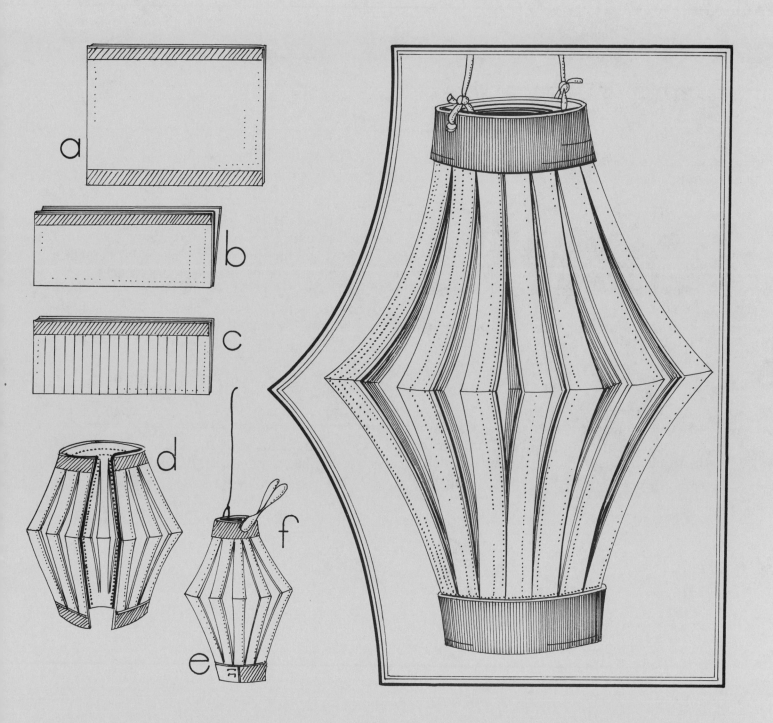

a

b

c

d

f

e

Dancing Dragon Mask

A dragon hanging on the wall,
Staring in a trance,
Comes alive when taken down,
To do his scary dance.

THINGS YOU NEED — pencil, colored paper, scissors, Ping-Pong ball, black poster paint, brush, glue, yarn, tape, aluminum foil

1. Draw a heart shape on a large piece of yellow paper; see light area in Fig. a. Cut out the heart.
*2. Cut a Ping-Pong ball in half with scissors, Fig. b. Paint both halves with black poster paint.
3. Glue each half to a white paper circle for eyes, Fig. c.
4. Glue the eyes to the top of the heart.
5. Cut out a nose and teeth shapes, similar to the ones shown in the drawing. Glue them to the heart below eyes, Fig. d.
6. Cut colored yarn into equal lengths.

7. Turn the heart over. Glue or tape the lengths of yarn evenly spaced to the bottom (pointed end), Fig. e.
8. Draw a crown shape on a piece of orange paper. Cut out the crown; see light area in Fig. f.
9. Glue the crown to the top of the heart on the back, Fig. g.
10. Cut five large red ovals. Cut a V into one end of each; see shaded area in Fig. h.
11. Study Fig. i and glue two ovals, V-cut facing up, near the top of the heart on the back.
12. Study Fig. j and glue two ovals, V-cut facing out, overlapping the first two ovals slightly.
13. Study Fig. k and glue the remaining oval at the bottom of the heart, with the V-cut facing down.
14. Glue or tape colored yarn to the three bottom ovals, Fig. l. Cut out small aluminum circles and glue them around the outer edge of the dragon.
15. Hang the mask on the wall for decoration. During the party take it down and do a silly dragon dance for your guests.

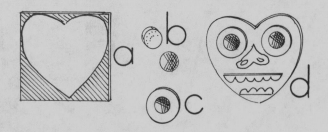

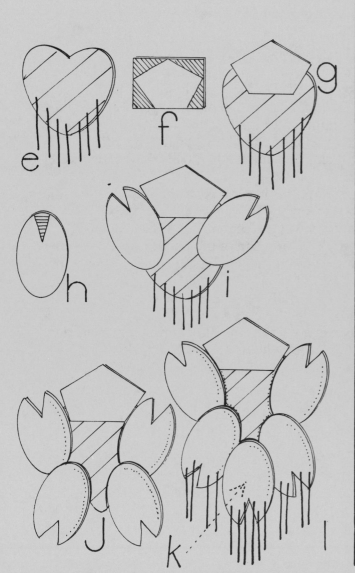

e f g

h i

j k l

Paper Blow Favors

Blow real hard into this toy,
And you will quickly learn,
That it will roll out very stiff,
Then soon it will return.

THINGS YOU NEED — scissors, lightweight paper (typewriter paper), beading wire or thin wire, glue, feathers, pencil

1. Cut a very long and narrow rectangle from lightweight paper. Fold in half and open again, Fig. a.

*2. Cut a length of wire a little shorter than the length of the paper, Fig. b.

3. Place the wire in the center of the bottom half of the folded paper, Fig. b. The wire should touch one short end of the paper.

4. Squeeze a narrow line of glue along the bottom edge of the paper below the wire, Fig. c.

5. Fold the top half of the paper over the glued bottom half, Fig. d. Let dry.

6. Fold the end of the paper, where the wire is touching, over a feather. Glue down, Fig. e. Let dry.

7. Fold both corners of the other end of the paper slightly, but leave a little bit of the edge unfolded at the center, Fig. f. Glue down.

8. Wrap the end of the paper with the feather in it around a pencil, Fig. g. Roll the paper tightly around the pencil, Fig. h.

9. Carefully remove the pencil.

10. Hold the end with the folded corners between your fingers. Blow through the opening. The paper will unroll and coil back.

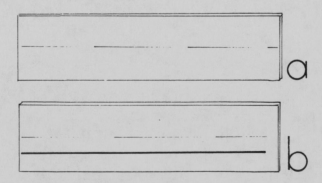

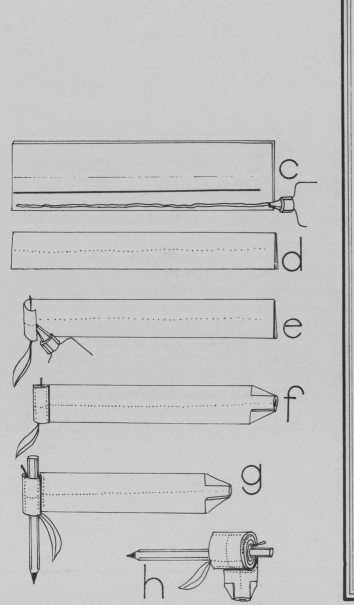

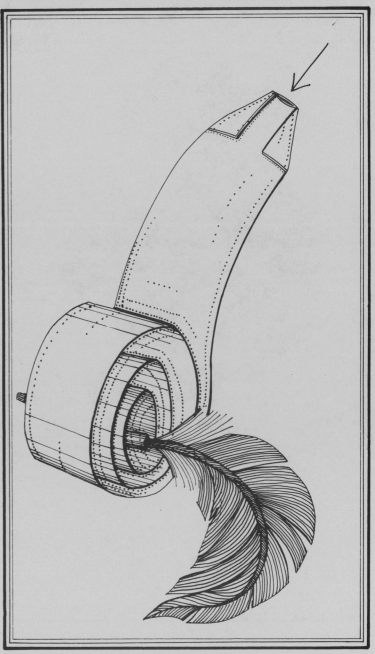

Bing-Banger Noisemaker

Put this toy between your hands
And spin it very fast.
It'll make a lot of noise
To last and last and last.

THINGS YOU NEED — corrugated cardboard, compass, scissors, crayons or markers,
pencil, string, beads or small metal washers,
plastic drinking straws or pencils, glue

*1. Draw a circle on corrugated cardboard with
a compass. Cut out.

2. Draw a smiling face on one side, Fig.a, and a
sad face on the other. Make sure the wavy
inside design of the cardboard is at the top and
bottom.
*3. Make two holes on opposite sides of the
cardboard with a sharp pencil, using a twisting
motion, Fig. b. The holes should be near the
edge.
4. Cut two lengths of string as long as the distance from one side of the circle to the other.
5. Tie a large bead or a small metal washer to
one end of each string.
6. Push the other end of the string through a
hole in the cardboard and make a knot, Fig. c.
7. Push the point of a pencil or a plastic drinking straw through the wavy inside cardboard
below the face, Fig. d. If you use a straw, a dab
of glue will keep it in place.
8. To work the noisemaker, hold the pencil or
straw between the palms of your hands. Roll the
pencil or straw first to the left and then to the
right. The faster you roll, the harder the beads
or washers will bang against the cardboard
head.

Tilting Scribe Game

A scribe with a serious face,
And a nicely well-rounded base,
Is spun by his hat,
Goes this way and that,
And stops when it's through in a space.

THINGS YOU NEED—three-inch foam ball, plastic knife, rock, white glue, foam cup, colored paper, scissors, tape, crayons or markers, ruler

*1. Carefully hollow out a foam ball using a plastic knife. Be sure not to cut too deep or you may break through the wall, Fig. a.

2. Place a rock inside the ball, Fig. b. The ball is shown as if you could see through it.

3. Pour glue into the ball around the stone, making sure the hole stays on top, Fig. b. Let dry.

4. Wrap a foam cup in colored paper, Fig. c.

5. Tape the paper in place, Fig. d.

6. Trim away the excess paper at the top and bottom of the cup.

7. Draw the scribe's face on the front of the wrapped cup with crayon or marker, Fig. e.

8. Squeeze glue around the bottom edge of the cup, Fig. f.

9. Place the glued edge directly over the hole of the ball, Fig. g. The cup should stand straight on the ball.

10. Cut a very large paper circle.

11. Divide the circle into many sections with a ruler and crayon, Fig. h. Write stunts and activities in each section.

12. To play the game, a player spins the scribe in the center of the circle. The player must act out the stunt or activity the scribe stops on.

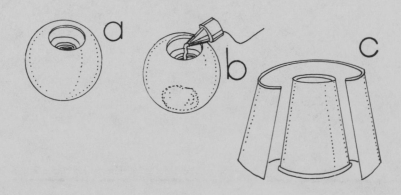

Little Added Extras

A. Fortune Cookies

1. Buy a package of plain, round cookies.
2. Cut thin strips of paper. Write a fortune on each strip. Fold the paper over to cover the writing.
3. Place the paper across one cookie.
4. Add a dab of jam to each side of the cookie. Avoid getting jelly on the paper.
5. Place a second cookie over the first and press down gently.

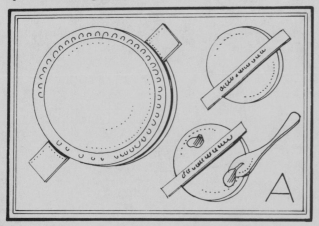

3. Cover a cookie sheet with waxed paper and drop spoonfuls of the chocolate-coated noodles on the paper.
4. Place the cookie sheet in a cool place or in a refrigerator so the drops will harden.

C. Party Tea

Make a pitcher of iced tea or, if you prefer, serve apple juice in cups, which looks very much like Chinese tea.

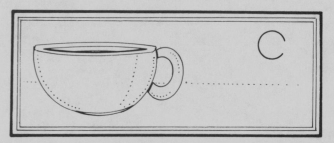

B. Noodle Drops

*1. Melt a package of chocolate bits in a pot over a low flame. Remove from the heat.
2. Add chow mein noodles into the melted chocolate. Stir well.

And don't forget the confetti!

Italian Puppet Party

Puppet shows are very popular in many parts of Italy. In Sicily they are presented in the home. Life-sized puppets (the Italian word is "pupi"), worked by rods, entertain the children. The show turns into a party when food and beverages are served.

When it's your birthday invite your friends to a festive Italian puppet show party. Turn your home into a puppet theater and your dining room into a stage. After the hero slays the dragon and saves the heroine, treat everyone to a piece of the stage, the stage cake, that is. Serve Italian favorites such as spumoni and a make-believe cappuccino. When it's time for your guests to leave, wave them off with a hearty "ciao" (pronounced "chow," it means good-bye in Italian).

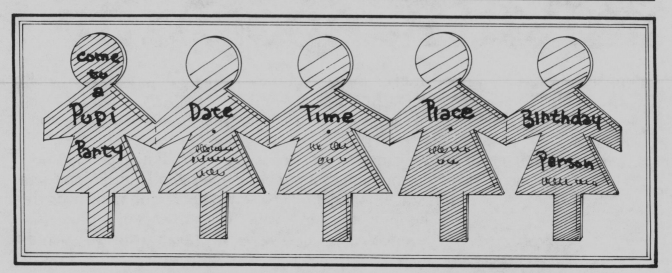

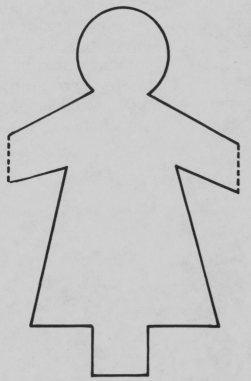

Puppet Invitations

Paper puppets ask each guest
To your puppet birthday fest.

THINGS YOU NEED—tracing paper, pencil, scissors, colored paper, markers or crayons

1. Trace the puppet shape from this book onto a sheet of tracing paper.
2. Cut out the tracing for a pattern.
3. Cut a very long rectangle from colored paper, as high as the puppet pattern.
4. Fold the paper evenly back and forth, making the folds as wide as the pattern. Use up all the paper.
5. Place the pattern on the folded paper. Trace around it with a pencil. The hands (dotted lines) are on the folded sides of the paper.
6. Cut out the traced puppet. Do not cut the

hands along the folded sides.

7. Write the party information on the row of puppets with a crayon or marker.

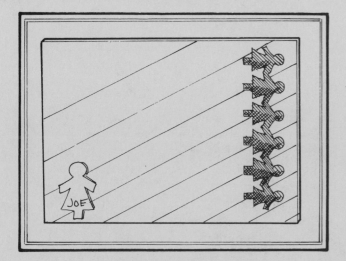

Puppet Place Mats

Names on place mats let all know
Where to sit for food and show.

THINGS YOU NEED—scissors, large sheets of colored paper, glue, crayons or markers

1. Cut a row of attached puppets just as you did for the invitations.
2. Glue the puppets to one short side of a large paper rectangle.
3. Cut off a single puppet from the chain for a placecard. Write the name of a guest on it with a crayon or marker.

Puppet Place Settings

Place setting puppets gaily dressed,
One for every party guest.

THINGS YOU NEED—scissors, colored paper, pencil, paper punch, yarn, plastic spoons and forks

1. Cut a dress shape from colored paper. Follow the pattern from the book, only remove the head and bottom piece, Fig. a.
2. Punch two holes at the top of the dress with a paper punch, Fig. b.
3. Weave a length of yarn through the holes. Tie the dress to a spoon, which is placed over a fork.

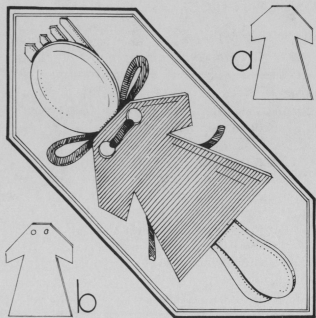

Theater Cake and Puppets

This cake, shaped like a theater stage
Even comes complete
With tasty icing scenery,
A perfect showtime treat.

THINGS YOU NEED—cake mix, two square cake pans, cookie sheet, aluminum foil, plastic knife, two packages of white frosting mix, gel icing in a tube, scissors, colored paper, toothpicks, glue, crepe paper or tissue paper, crayons or markers, string

A. Theater Cake

1. Bake a cake in two square baking pans. Follow package directions. Remove from the pans and let cool.
2. Cover a cookie sheet with aluminum foil.
3. Cut one cake into two pieces, one slightly larger than the other, Fig. a.
4. Mix two boxes of white frosting mix, according to package directions.
5. Arrange the two cut sections of cake against the uncut cake, Fig. b. Put a little frosting in between sections to hold the ends in place.
6. Frost the cake, except the top of the uncut cake, with a plastic knife. This will be the stage floor.
7. Decorate the front of the larger standing section with gel icing in tube. This is the scenery for the theater.
8. Decorate the sides and end of the cake with fancy designs.

B. Cake Puppets

1. Cut two small circles for each puppet head from colored paper. Draw a face on one circle with a crayon or marker.
2. Glue the two circles together with the wide end of a flat toothpick between them, Fig. c.
3. Cut a long, narrow length of colored crepe paper or tissue paper for a skirt.
4. Place the toothpick over one end of the paper, Fig. d.
5. Gather the paper loosely around the toothpick, under the head, Fig. e.
6. Tie the gathered paper to the toothpick with a piece of string, under the head, Fig. f.

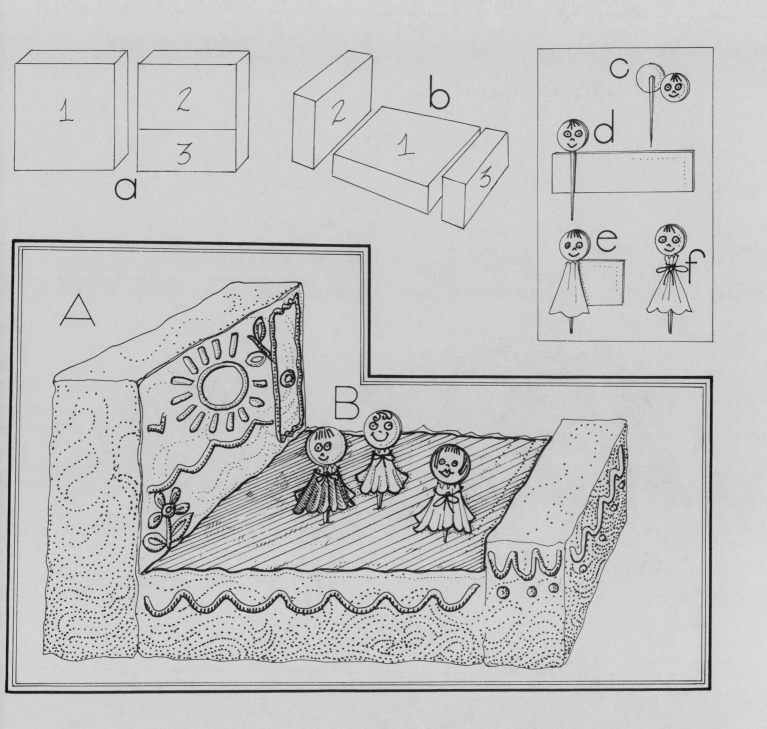

Jing-Jingly Tamborine Favors

Make a favor for each guest,
Which helps to set the scene.
Dance to music from this gift,
A jingly tamborine.

THINGS YOU NEED—candies, small paper plates, aluminum foil, scissors, stapler, ribbon

1. Place candies on a paper plate, Fig. a.
2. Place another paper plate over it, Fig. b.

3. Cut small circles from aluminum foil.
4. Place small circles around the rim of the top plate. Staple it in place through both plates, Fig. c. If your candies are really small, add extra staples close together.
5. Staple several circles to both plates, around the rim. Leave a small space without a circle.
6. Cut several lengths of different colored ribbons.
7. Gather the ribbons and staple them to the small space between the circles, Fig. d.

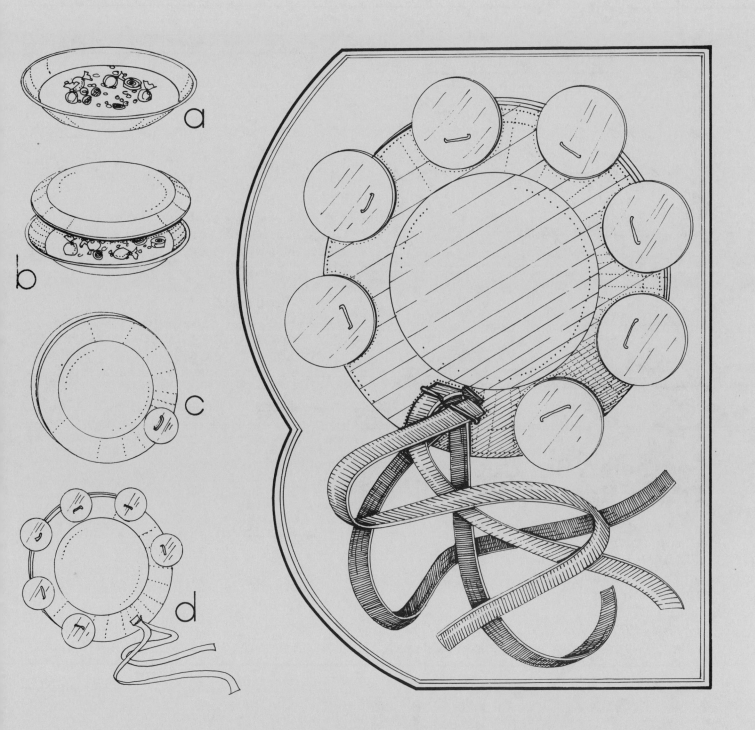

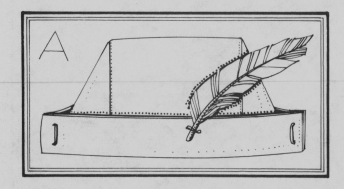

A. Feathered Hat

1. Fold a large sheet of colored paper in half along the longer side, Fig. a.
2. Fold the two corners of the folded edge over, Fig. b.
3. Fold the paper below the folded corners (fold only one thickness) up and over the corners, Fig. c.
4. Turn the hat over and fold the remaining paper up, in line with the opposite side, Fig. d.
5. Staple the two ends together.
6. Staple a feather to the side of the hat.

B. Flower Headband

1. Cut flower shapes from colored paper.
2. Punch two holes near the center of each flower with a paper punch.
3. Cut a narrow ribbon long enough to tie around a head.
4. Weave several flowers on the ribbon.

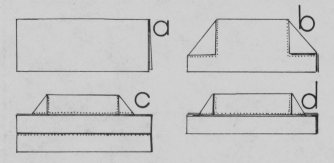

Feathered Hat and Flower Headband

There once was a young man named Joe,
Who had a cute girlfriend named Flo,
Dressed in flowers and feather,
In sunshiny weather,
They went to the best puppet show.

THINGS YOU NEED—large sheets of colored paper, stapler, feathers, scissors, paper punch, narrow ribbon

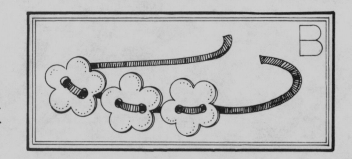

Folk Art Window Banners

In towns of northern Italy,
Near mountains very tall,
These shades are hung from window panes,
Admired by one and all.

THINGS YOU NEED — scissors, large sheets of colored paper, pencil, glue, crayons or markers

1. Cut out a simple vase shape, similar to the one shown in the drawing, from colored paper. Make it large enough to hold a bouquet of flowers.
2. Glue the shape near the bottom of a large sheet of colored paper.
3. Cut flower and leaf shapes from colored paper.
4. Draw flower stems coming out of the glued shape with a crayon or marker. See the drawing for some designs.
5. Glue the flowers and leaves to the drawn stems.
6. Hang several banners around the party room.

Pinocchio Centerpiece

Pinocchio, as the old story goes,
Made of wood from his head to his toes,
Had innocent eyes,
But told lots of lies,
Which caused him to grow a long nose.

THINGS YOU NEED — three cardboard bathroom tissue tubes, scissors, poster paints, brush, pencil, tape, colored paper, string, two large beads, glue, Ping-Pong ball, plastic drinking straw, markers, three large plastic bottle caps.

*1. Cut two deep V shapes into one end of a cardboard toilet tissue tube, opposite each other, with a scissors, Fig. a.

2. Paint the tube with green poster paint, Fig. b. Paint a second, uncut tube, red.

3. Place one end of the uncut tube on red paper. Trace around it, Fig. c. Cut out the traced circle.

4. Tape the uncut tube to the cut tube, Fig. d. The V cuts are at the bottom.

*5. Make two holes opposite each other near the top edge of the tube, with a sharp pencil, using a twisting motion, Fig. e.

6. Knot one end of a length of string. Add a bead to the string, resting on the knot.

7. Push the unknotted end of the string through both holes on the tube, Fig. f.

8. Add a bead to the extending string, Fig. f. Knot the end of the string to keep the bead in place.

9. Glue the cut circle to the top tube, Fig. f.

10. Cut two small squares of red paper and roll them into long, narrow cones, Fig. g. Tape in place, Fig. h.

11. Trim the bottom of each cone so they fit over the beads.

12. Glue the cones to the beads for arms, Fig. i.

13. Roll red paper into a wide cone hat, large enough to fit over a Ping-Pong ball. Tape and trim, Fig. j.

*14. Carefully make a hole in a Ping-Pong ball with a sharp pencil, using a twisting motion, Fig. k.

15. Glue the cone to the Ping-Pong ball, Fig. 1.

16. Glue a short piece of a plastic drinking straw into the hole for a long nose, Fig. m.

17. Draw a face on the ball with a marker.

18. Glue the bottom of a bottle cap to the red circle on the top tube. Glue the head to the cap.

19. Cut two shoe shapes from paper rectangles, Fig. n.

20. Glue the bottom of a bottle cap to each shoe, Fig. o.

21. Push Pinocchio's legs into the caps.

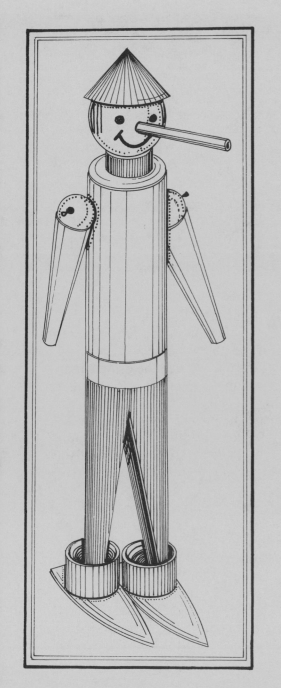

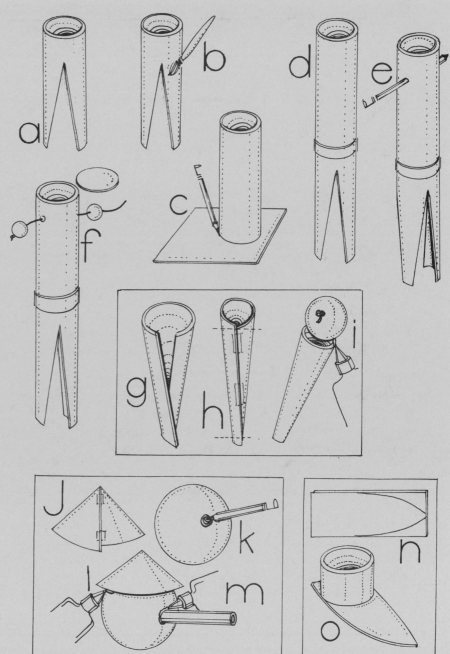

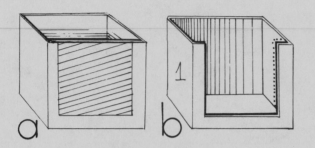

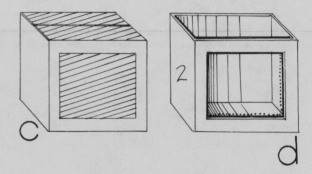

Puppet Theater

A puppet dancing on a string,
Gay or in a rage,
Will dance or sway or jump around
On its cardboard stage.

THINGS YOU NEED—scissors, three cartons all the same size, pencil, ruler, wide masking tape, poster paint, brush, colored paper, crayons or markers, colored poster board (oaktag)

*1. Cut away the open top flaps, if any, and the bottom of a carton.

2. Draw a line a little way from the bottom and sides on a long side of a carton, with a pencil or ruler; study Fig. a.

*3. Cut out the area between the lines, Fig. b (shaded area in Fig. a). This is the top of the theater (1).

*4. Cut away the open top flaps, if any, of a second carton. Leave the bottom on.

5. Draw a line a little way from all the edges of one long side of the carton; study Fig. c.

*6. Cut away the area between the drawn lines, Fig. d (shaded area in Fig. c). This is the stage of the theater (2).

*7. Cut away the open top flaps, if any, of the third carton. This is the bottom of the theater.

8. Place the three cartons one on top of the other, Fig. e. Tape together. Fig. f shows you the back view of the taped boxes.

9. Paint the theater with poster paints. Add designs similar to the ones in the drawing.

10. Cut paper to fit against the back inside wall of the stage. Draw designs on it with a crayon or marker for the scenery. Change scenery between acts.

11. Cut a piece of colored oaktag to fit in front of the stage for a curtain. Remove and replace between acts.

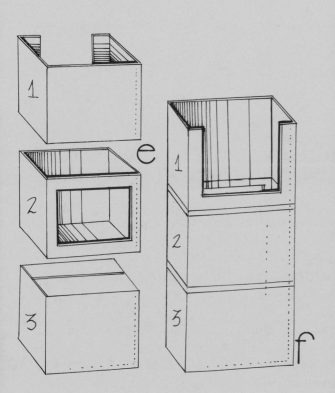

e

f

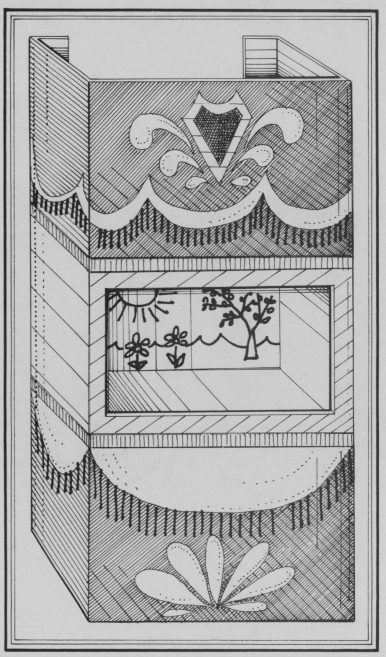

Theater Puppets

To go with your theater,
Its stage and handsome sets,
You need some special puppets –
A cast of marionettes.

THINGS YOU NEED—scissors, colored paper, cardboard bathroom tissue tubes, tape, white tissue paper, Ping-Pong balls, pencil, crayons or markers, glue, yarn, cotton, cord, paper clips, crepe paper, paper punch

1. Cut colored paper as high as a cardboard bathroom tissue tube. It should be long enough to wrap around the tube plus a little extra.
2. Wrap the paper around a tube, Fig. a. Tape in place, Fig. b.
*3. Carefully make a hole completely through a Ping-Pong ball with a sharp pencil, using a twisting motion, Fig. c.
4. Cut several squares of white tissue paper large enough to wrap around a Ping-Pong ball plus a little extra.
5. Make a hole with a pencil through the center of the stacked tissue.
6. Tie one end of a long piece of cord or yarn to a paper clip.
7. Push the other end of the yarn through the holes of the ball, then through the hole in the tissues, Fig. d.
8. Bring the sides of the tissue around the ball and twist them together above the paper clip, Fig. e.
9. Glue the head to the top of the tube, with the ends of the tissue tucked inside, Fig. f.
10. Cut two arm and two shoe shapes from colored paper.
11. Glue the arms to the sides of the tube. Glue the shoes to the bottom (inside) of the tube, Fig. g.
12. Decorate the puppet body with paper cutouts or crayon designs.
13. Make a cast of puppets, similar to the ones shown in the drawing.
14. Cut lengths of crepe paper for capes (short) or for dresses (long).
15. Punch holes with a paper punch along one long side of the crepe or tissue paper, Fig. h.
16. Feed a length of yarn through the holes, Fig. i.
17. Tie the cape or dress to the top of the puppet's body, using cord or yarn, Fig. j.
18. Stand behind the open back of the top carton. Drop the puppets onto the stage by the strings for the play.

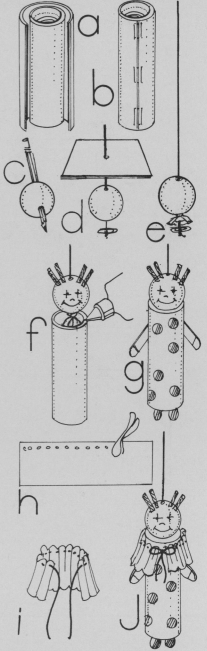

Little Added Extras

A. The Meatball Game
1. Color a Ping-Pong ball with a red marker.
2. Hit the ball from player to player with Ping-Pong paddles. You can use large cardboard rectangles if you don't have paddles. Whoever misses is out of the game. Last person wins.

B. Spumoni Ice Cream
1. Check your supermarket for spumoni ice cream. If you can't find any, lemon and orange sherbet are two other Italian favorites. Or you can buy vanilla ice cream and sprinkle it with candied fruits.
2. Make Italian flags from small white paper rectangles, the left side green and the right side red. (The middle stripe is white.) Glue the flags to toothpicks.
3. Scoop ice cream on a plate and add a flag.

C. Kids' Cappuccino
1. Pour chocolate milk into coffee mugs and add a scoop of coffee ice cream. Top with a dab of whipped cream.
2. Tie colored yarn into a bow around the top of a drinking straw.

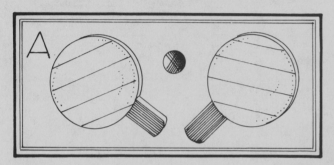

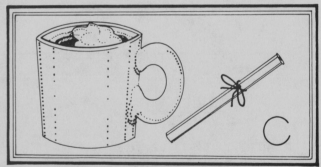

And don't forget the confetti!

Hawaiian Luau Party

Hawaii is a tropical paradise with green mountains, deep blue sky, and sandy beaches. Unless you live there, it is hard to imagine just how beautiful the islands are. On Hawaii friends gather for a big party called a luau. People sit on tiny flat stools by low tables. They feast on pig, fish, poi, coconuts, pineapples, and bananas. Poi, a mash made from a native root, is a popular starchy food.

Since your birthday is coming soon, why not bring Hawaii to your home and throw a luau birthday party. Decorate the room with flowers, vines, and tropical fruit. When your guests arrive, welcome them to your luau with a friendly "Aloha." Give each guest an evil tiki mask. No luau party is complete without dancers in grass skirts doing the hula. It will be an enchanting time for sure.

Lei Invitations

On a bright Hawaiian lei
Announce your luau's time and day.

THINGS YOU NEED — scissors, paper punch, colored paper, crayons or markers, string

1. Cut small flower shapes from colored paper, similar to the ones shown in the drawing.
2. Punch two holes close to each other near the center of each flower with a paper punch.
3. Write the party information on the flowers with a crayon or marker.
4. Weave a length of string through the holes in the flowers. Knot the ends of the string.

Flower Place Mats and Place Settings

When it's time to sit and eat
Put a place mat by each seat.

THINGS YOU NEED — large sheets of colored paper, compass, scissors, glue

1. Draw a large circle on colored paper with a compass.
2. Cut a scalloped design around the edge of the circle.
3. Cut out a small circle and glue it to the center of the scalloped circle.
4. Cut small flower shapes from colored paper similar to the one shown in the drawing.
5. Make a slit into the flower to the center, then cut out a small circle from the center.
6. Slip a fork and spoon through the slit and into the center opening.

Vine Decorations

Make a pretty trailing vine,
So tropical in feeling,
It adds a lovely luau touch,
Entwined across the ceiling.

THINGS YOU NEED—scissors, package of green crepe paper, green crepe paper ribbon, tape

1. Cut the crepe paper across the shorter side, creating several wide strips, Fig. a.
2. Cut a wavy design into both long sides of each strip, Fig. b. Do not cut the folded ends.
3. Unfold the wavy strips. They will look like long vines.
4. String long pieces of crepe paper ribbon across the party room. Tape the vines to the ribbons.

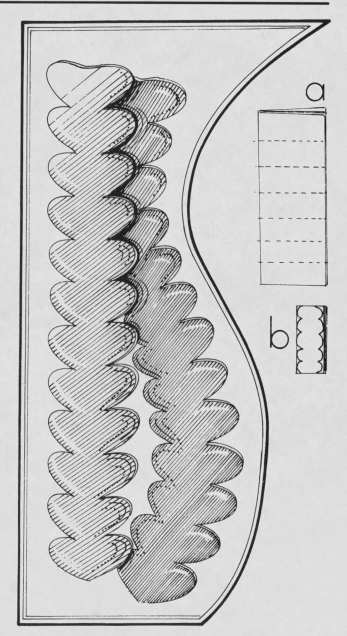

Flower Basket Cake

Place some pretty flowers
In the center of your cake.
When the party's over,
A flower each guest will take.

THINGS YOU NEED — angel cake mix, angel cake pan or two round cake pans, cardboard circle, aluminum foil, yellow frosting mix, plastic knife, dark gel icing in a tube, scissors, colored tissue or crepe paper, sharp pencil, plastic drinking straws, string

*1. Bake a cake in an angel cake pan, Fig. a. Follow package directions. (If you do not have this type of cake pan, bake it in two round cake pans.) Remove from the pan and let cool.

2. Place the cake on a cardboard circle that has been covered with aluminum foil.

3. Mix the frosting, following package directions, and spread it on the sides of the cake with a plastic knife. Do not frost the top of the cake, Fig. b. (If you have made two round cakes, put them together with a little frosting between the layers before you frost the sides. *Cut a hole into the center of the cakes with a knife.)

4. Make slanted lines completely around the side of the cake with dark gel icing in a tube, Fig. c.

5. Draw more slanted lines around the cake, crisscrossing the first lines.

6. Cut three different-sized circles from colored tissue or crepe paper.

7. Cut a wavy design around the edge of the circles, Fig. d.

8. Place the three circles centered on top of each other. The largest circle is at the bottom.

9. Make a hole in the center of all three circles with a sharp pencil, Fig. e.

10. Push one end of a plastic drinking straw through the holes of the circles, the large circle first, Fig. f.

11. Bring the circles up over the end of the straw, Fig. g.

12. Tie the bottom of the circles tightly to the straw with a small piece of string, Fig. h.

13. Fluff the circles to form a flower. Make several.

14. Put the straw ends of the flowers into the hole of the cake.

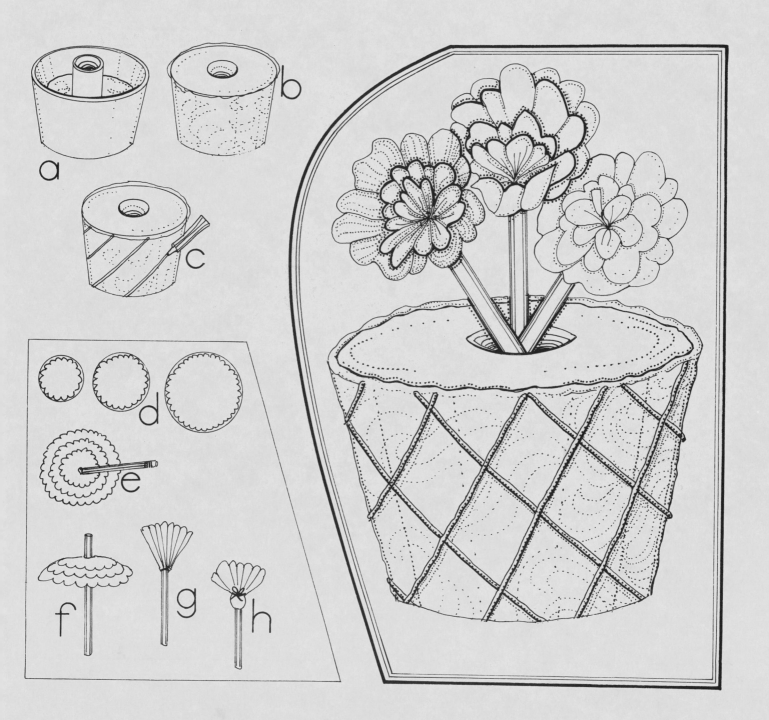

a

b

c

d

e

f

g

h

Basket of Flowers Favors

These baskets of flowers
Are really big treats.
There's a secret inside —
They're filled up with sweets.

THINGS YOU NEED — scissors, quart-sized milk carton, colored paper, tape, crayons or markers, glue, wrapped candies

1. Cut a quart-sized carton to the height you want your basket to be, Fig. a.
2. Cut a piece of colored paper as high as the bottom of the carton and long enough to wrap around it plus a little extra.
3. Wrap the paper around the carton and tape in place, Figs. b and c.
4. Draw designs on the four sides with crayons or markers, Fig. d.
5. Cut circles from colored paper. Cut a wavy design around the edge of each circle. Cut long rectangle stems, Fig. e.
6. Glue the flowers to the stems, Fig. f.
7. Glue the stems to the inside of the carton, on all four sides, Fig. g. (Each favor should have a friend's name on one of the flowers stems.)
8. Fill the basket with party candies.

a

b

c

d

e

f

g

Jonathan

Fun Fruit Centerpiece

A girl from Hawaii named Anna
Carried around a bandanna,
She filled it with fruit,
So when hungry en route,
She could munch on a yellow banana.

THINGS YOU NEED—scissors, colored paper, round cardboard container (from salt, oatmeal, etc.), crayons or markers, tape, pencil, glue

1. Cut a piece of yellow or orange paper as high as a round cardboard container. It should be long enough to wrap around it plus a little extra.

2. Draw lines crisscrossing each other on the paper with crayons or markers. Color small triangles inside each diamond, Fig. a.

3. Wrap the paper around the container, Fig. b. Tape in place, Fig. c.

4. Place the container on a piece of yellow or orange paper. Trace around the bottom with a pencil, Fig. d.

5. Cut out the traced circle.

6. Glue the circle to the top of the container, Fig. e.

7. Draw long leaf shapes on green paper rectangles. Draw a vein design with a crayon or marker, Fig. f. Make six leaves.

8. Cut out the leaves.

9. Make a hole in the center of the covered end of the container with a sharp pencil, using a twisting motion, Fig. g. The hole should be large enough to put your thumb into.

10. Stack several leaves on top of each other, lining up the ends.

11. Roll the stacked leaves at the bottom. Slip the rolled ends into the hole, Fig. h.

12. Fluff out the leaves. Display the pineapple with some artificial fruit.

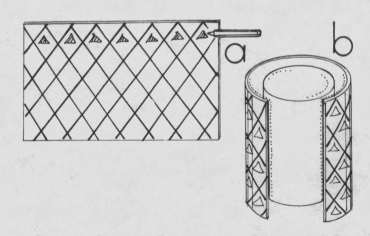

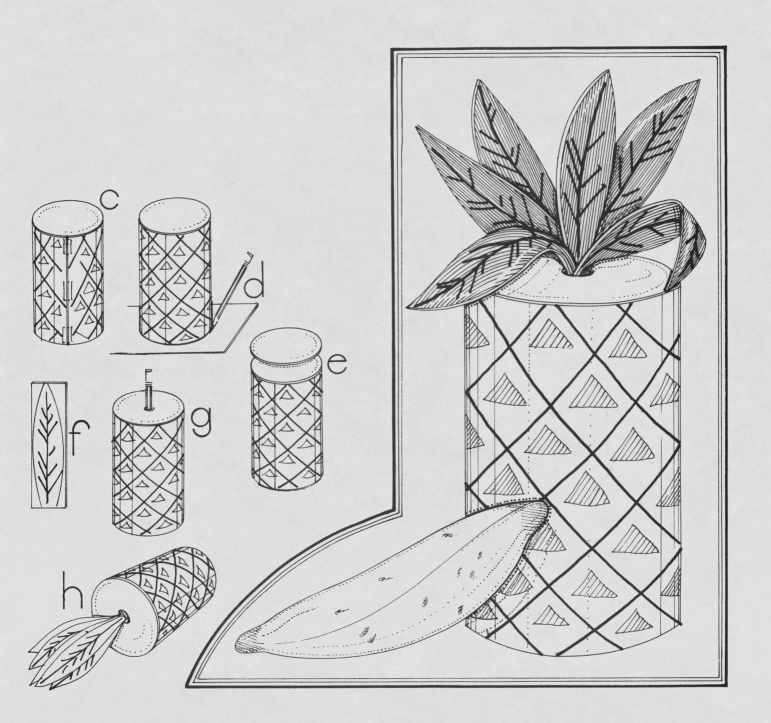

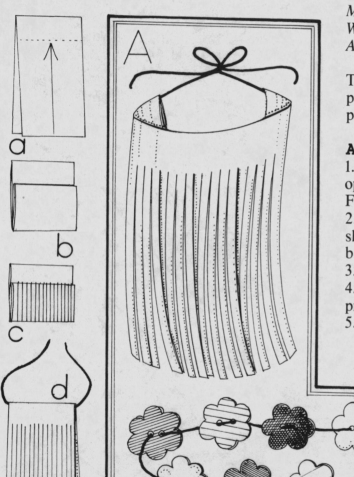

Aloha Grass Skirt and Flowery Lei

To do a graceful hula dance,
Make your body sway.
Wear a special hula skirt,
And don't forget the lei!

THINGS YOU NEED—package of crepe paper, scissors, cord or yarn, colored paper, paper punch

A. Grass Skirt
1. Unfold a package of crepe paper. Fold the open paper in half across the shorter side, Fig. a.
2. Fold the paper again, bringing the ends a short distance away from the folded edge, Fig. b; see arrow and dotted line in Fig. a.
3. Cut slits into the folded area, Fig. c.
4. Unfold the paper and drape it over a long piece of cord or yarn, Fig. d.
5. Tie the skirt around your waist.

B. Lei
1. Cut small flower shapes from colored paper.
2. Punch two holes near the center of each flower.
3. String the flowers on a long piece of yarn. Tie the ends into a knot.
4. Wear the lei around your neck.

Tiki Masks

Every guest who comes today
Will get a tiki face,
To chase the evil spirits,
And to keep them in their place.

THINGS YOU NEED — scissors, colored paper, pencil, crayons or markers, glue, feathers, sequins, stapler, plastic drinking straws

1. Cut a rectangle as wide as your head (from side to side) from colored paper. It should be as high as the distance from your nose to your forehead.
2. Draw two ovals on the paper with a pencil. Overlap them at the center of the paper, Fig. a.
3. Draw a small oval centered inside each oval, Fig. b.
4. Cut out the ovals, following the outer lines.
5. Cut out the smaller ovals for the eyes.
6. Decorate with a crayon or marker. Glue on feathers and sequins.
7. Staple a drinking straw to one end of the oval, at the back of the mask, Fig. c.

Sleeping Volcano Game

Throw Ping-Pong balls at the volcano
Sitting on the floor
If you get one in its opening
You will make a score.

THINGS YOU NEED—poster board (oak-tag), tape, scissors, glue, cotton, green tissue paper, colored paper, cardboard bathroom tissue tube, corrugated cardboard, Ping-Pong balls

1. Roll a sheet of poster board into a cone and tape, Fig. a. The top point should have an opening at least twice the size of a Ping-Pong ball.

2. Trim the top and bottom edges of the cone to form circles. This is the volcano.

3. Glue cotton around the top opening for clouds. Glue balls of crumpled green tissue paper around the bottom for bushes, Fig. b.

4. Cut brown paper high and wide enough to wrap around a cardboard bathroom tissue tube. Tape in place, Fig. c.

5. Cut long leaf shapes from green paper rectangles, Fig. d. Make several.

6. Push a bunch of leaves into one end of the tube, Fig. e. Arrange the leaves to look like the top of a palm tree, Fig. f. Make several palm trees.

7. Cover a large piece of corrugated cardboard with green paper. You can also paint it green.

8. Place the volcano in the center of the green cardboard.

9. Cut a blue paper lake. Tape or glue it in front of the volcano.

10. Glue or tape the trees plus a few more bushes made from crumpled green tissue paper around the volcano.

11. Cut flame shapes from red paper. Tape them inside the top opening, at the back.

12. To play the game, each player gets five Ping-Pong balls. Each tosses the balls from a measured distance and tries to get them inside the volcano through the top hole. The player who gets the most balls inside the volcano is the winner.

Dancing Poles and Drums

When the drums begin to play,
It's every dancer's goal
To quickly move her feet away
From each colliding pole.

THINGS YOU NEED — cardboard tubes (paper towel or bathroom tissue), masking tape, round cardboard containers (salt, oatmeal, etc.), colored paper, crayons or markers

A. Dancing Poles

1. Tape cardboard tubes together with masking tape to form two very long poles.
2. To do a Hawaiian dance, two people hold the ends of the poles in their hands. While kneeling first they bang the poles together on the floor, and then they slowly separate them about two feet and bang them again on the floor. As this is happening, one or two dancers hop in and out of the poles, trying not to get their feet caught when the poles are banged together.

B. Drums

1. Cut colored paper large enough to wrap around the container.
2. Decorate the paper with a crayon or marker.
3. Tape the paper around the container.
4. With your fingertips, bang on several drums during the dance.

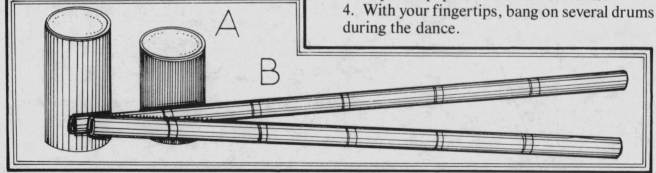

Little Added Extras

A. Tropical Refreshments

Serve pineapple juice over ice cubes. Cut orange slices as a garnish for your drink. Add a drop of fruit sherbet or serve it separately.

B. Fruit Starburst

1. Cut away one-third of a cabbage or hard lettuce.
2. Wrap the remainder of the head in aluminum foil.
3. Cut fruit (fresh or canned) into bite-sized pieces.
4. Insert a toothpick into each fruit. Push the toothpicks into the cabbage or lettuce.

C. Twirling Balls

*1. Using a twisting motion, make a hole through the center of two foam balls with a pencil.

2. Push one end of a long piece of cord or yarn through each ball. Knot the end around a paper clip.
3. A dancer holds the yarn and twirls the balls around. Someone can play the drum while the dancer twirls the balls.

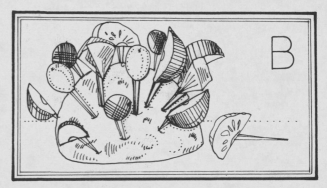

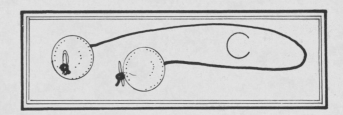

And don't forget the confetti!

Holiday Parties

Did you ever wonder why a particular day became a holiday? Well, a holiday is a day set aside to honor something or someone special.

Here are seven special holiday parties to celebrate with your friends and family. Circle the dates on your calendar and get busy preparing for the first one to come along.

Be My Valentine Party

Valentine's Day is the holiday for remembering the people you love or care about. Be a Cupid and celebrate this holiday with a party. Invite all of your favorite people and give them a piece of your heart, a heart cake, that is. Make "Love" pins for everyone and decorate your home with Valentine's flowers, and hanging birds. This will be a day your friends will remember in their hearts forever.

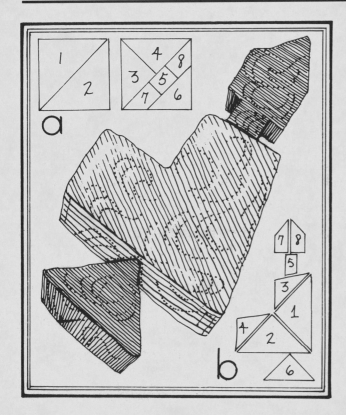

Follow package directions. Remove from the pans and let cool.

2. Cut the two cakes as shown in Fig. a.

3. Cover a cookie sheet with aluminum foil.

4. Arrange all of pieces of cake on the cookie sheet, as shown in Fig. b. All pieces should be touching each other.

5. Mix the white frosting according to package directions. Add red food coloring to the white frosting. Use this to frost the heart part of the cake with a plastic knife.

6. Mix the chocolate frosting. Frost the arrow part of the cake.

Be My Valentine Cake

Here's a cake to slice apart—
Cupid's arrow through a heart.

THINGS YOU NEED—cake mix, two square cake pans, plastic knife, cookie sheet, aluminum foil, white and chocolate frosting mixes, food coloring

1. Bake a cake mix in two square cake pans.

Sweetheart Punch

1. Put red sour balls or red gel candy into the compartments of ice cube trays. Fill with water and freeze.

2. Place the frozen cubes into cherry punch and serve with tiny red-hot cinnamon candy hearts.

Delicate Valentine Hearts

Make many hearts this special day,
And hang them from the ceiling.
These valentines will gently sway,
To add a loving feeling.

THINGS YOU NEED—white and colored paper, pencil, scissors, glue, paper punch, tape, string, small doily, sponge

A. Cut Paper Valentine

1. Fold a white paper rectangle in half.
2. Draw a half heart shape on the fold of the paper. Cut out along the drawn lines; see white area in Fig. a.
3. Cut a zigzag design along the edge of the half heart, through both layers, Fig. b. Do not cut the folded edge.
4. Draw a line on the paper, starting at the fold near the bottom point. Curve the line upward following the outer edge of the paper, as shown in Fig. b.
5. Cut along the drawn line.
6. Cut little rain drop shapes into the paper on the inside of the cut line, Fig. c.
7. Cut wavy shapes into the paper outside the cut line, Fig. d.

8. Open the paper.
9. Cut a heart from red paper; make it slightly smaller than the white heart. Glue it to the back. The red heart will show through the cuts on the white heart.

B. Hanging Punched Heart

1. Draw two hearts, the same size, on red squares of paper, Fig. e. Cut out the hearts.
2. Cut a slit from the top V to the center of one heart, Fig. f.
3. Cut a slit from the bottom point to the center of the other heart, Fig. g.
4. Punch holes around the edge of both hearts with a paper punch.
5. Fit the slit of one heart into the slit of the other, Fig. h.
6. Tape a length of string to the top of the assembled hearts. Hang the heart mobile.

C. Three-Dimensional Lace Heart

1. Cut a heart from red paper smaller than a doily.
2. Cut two tiny squares from a sponge.
3. Glue the square sponges to the back of the heart, one near the top and the other near the bottom. Let dry.
4. Squeeze glue on the sponges and glue the heart centered on the doily. Let dry.

Lovebird Mobile

Pretty paper lovebirds
Hang high above the ground.
Show your friends you really love
To have them come around.

THINGS YOU NEED—cardboard, compass, scissors, pencil, ruler, paper punch, colored paper, glue, red crayon, string, paper clip

1. Draw a large circle on cardboard with a compass. Cut out the circle.
2. Draw two lines crossing each other at the center, dividing the circle into four equal parts, Fig. a. Use a pencil and ruler.
*3. Punch a hole in the center of the circle with the point of the compass. Punch holes on the lines near the edge of the circle, Fig. a. (Be sure your hand is not underneath the circle.)
4. To make the birds, cut eight small squares of white paper.
5. Fold the squares in half. Draw a half heart shape on each folded square on the fold, Fig. b. Cut out along the drawn lines.
6. Open four of the hearts for the birds' bodies.

7. Cut two tiny triangles for each bird's beak, from yellow paper. Glue on to opposite sides of each heart, as shown in the drawing, Fig. c.
8. Refold the hearts. Draw a heart-shaped eye on both sides of the paper near the beak with a red crayon, Fig. d.
9. Punch a hole in the top of each folded heart with a paper punch; see top arrow in Fig. d.
10. Cut a slit, at an angle, into the fold of each folded heart near the top; see bottom arrow in Fig. d.
11. Open the remaining four hearts. Cut a short slit into the top V of each; see arrow in Fig. e.
12. Cut two feather shapes from pink paper for each heart. Glue a feather shape to each half of the hearts, Fig. e.
13. Refold the hearts with the feathers for wings.
14. Slip the slit of the folded wings into the slits of the folded bodies, Fig. f.
15. Cut four pieces of string all the same length. Knot one end into the hole in each of the birds.
16. Push the remaining end of each string through a hole in the circle near the edge. Tie each to the ring.
17. Cut a long piece of string. Push one end into the center hole and tie it to a paper clip. Hang the mobile by the string.

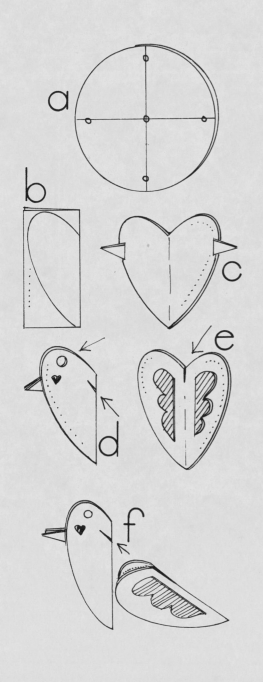

a

b

c

d

e

f

Basket of Hearts

Be sure to give your heart away,
To all your loves on Valentine's Day.

THINGS YOU NEED—colored paper, compass, scissors, pencil, ruler, glue, small metal can, salt, thin wire or pipe cleaners.

1. Draw a large circle on colored paper with a compass. Cut the circle out.
2. Mark the center of the circle, then draw two lines on either side of the center of the circle with a pencil and ruler, Fig. a. The lines should be the same distance from each other, and from the sides of the circle.
3. Draw two vertical lines in the center of the two horizontal lines to form a square, Fig. b.
4. Draw two crisscrossing lines, using a pencil and ruler from opposite points of the square through the center of the circle; see dotted lines in Fig. c.
5. Cut along the crisscrossing lines up to the center square; see dotted lines in Fig. c.
6. Fold the paper along the two long center lines, Fig. d.
7. Bring the section marked with an X in the drawing, up and over the center sections, Fig. e. Glue in place.
8. Fill a small metal can halfway with salt, Fig. f.
9. Cut small red and pink paper hearts. Glue each to a length of thin wire or a pipe cleaner, Fig. g.
10. Push the wires or pipe cleaners into the salt inside the can.
11. Place the can of hearts inside the paper basket.

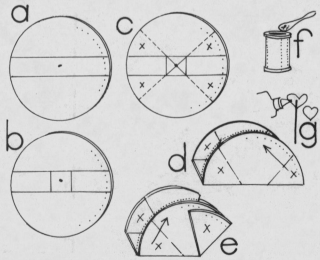

St. Patrick's Day Party

As the story goes, a teenager named Patrick was kidnapped by pirates and taken to Ireland as a slave. He was held captive for seven years before he escaped. Eventually, he became a priest and performed several miracles, for which he was made a saint. The most famous miracle was chasing the poisonous snakes from Ireland.

Today, you and your friends can be Irish for a day. Celebrate St. Patrick's Day by wearing something green. Make the boat that brought St. Patrick to Ireland. Have pots of shamrocks everywhere. Give every guest a pipe filled with delicious candies. Don't forget to have a few leprechauns close by and a shamrock in your hat for good luck.

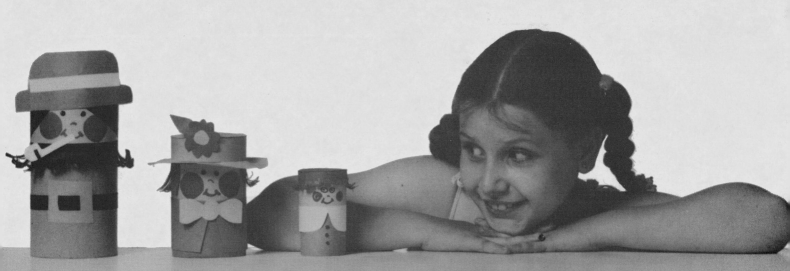

on several cookie sheets.

3. Fill each cone with batter a little less than half way.

4. Bake the cakes in a preheated 350-degree oven for 20 to 25 minutes. Remove and let cool.

5. Cut small shamrocks from green paper.

6. Glue a shamrock to the flat end of a toothpick. Make several.

7. Push several shamrocks into each cake.

Minty Limeade

1. Place a green spearmint-leaf candy into each compartment of an ice-cube tray. Add water and freeze.

2. Mix frozen limeade or lemonade, colored with green food coloring.

3. Put an ice cube into each glass of limeade.

Pot of Shamrocks Cakes

Atop these cakes, each guest will pluck,
A bunch of shamrocks, for good luck.

THINGS YOU NEED—chocolate cake mix, flat-bottomed ice cream cones, cookie sheets, scissors, green paper, toothpicks, glue

*1. Prepare a chocolate cake mix. Follow package directions.

2. Place thirty flat-bottomed ice cream cones

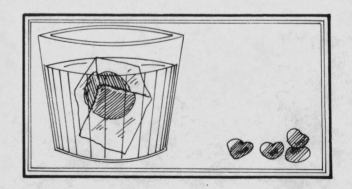

Erin Pipe Favors

Make these pipes and fill the bowls,
With candies for a favor.
Your friends will love this special treat,
So full of Irish flavor.

THINGS YOU NEED—poster paints, small paper cups (bathroom size), kitchen cleanser, brush, pencil, brown paper, scissors, plastic drinking straw, candies, glue, green ribbon

1. Mix white poster paint with a little kitchen cleanser in a paper cup. The cleanser added to the paint helps it stick to the cup.
2. Paint a small paper cup white.
3. Twist a sharp pencil completely through the cup at an angle, Fig. a.
4. Place the rim of the cup on brown paper. Trace around it with a pencil, Fig. b.
5. Cut out the traced circle.
6. Push a plastic drinking straw through the holes in the cup. Extend the straw slightly through the hole closest to the bottom of the cup, Fig. c.
7. Put candies in the cup.
8. Squeeze glue around the edge of the paper circle, Fig. d.
9. Press the glued circle to the rim of the cup, Fig. e. Let dry.
10. Tie a length of green ribbon around the long end of the straw.
11. For a play pipe, leave the pipe empty.

Leprechaun Family

A leprechaun's an Irish elf,
So small it's hardly seen.
Display this family on a shelf,
All dressed in kelly green.

THINGS YOU NEED—scissors, colored paper, large round cardboard container (oatmeal), small round container (salt, cleanser, etc.), cardboard bathroom tissue tube, tape, pencil, glue, crayons or markers

1. Cut three pieces of green paper: one as high as a large round container, one as high as a small round container, and one as high as a cardboard bathroom tissue tube. The paper should be long enough to wrap around the cylinder plus a little extra.
2. Wrap the paper around each and tape in place.
3. Place one end of each container and of the tube on green paper. Trace around each with a pencil.
4. Cut out the traced circles. Glue the circle to one end of its matching container and one to the tube. This end will be the top, Fig. a.
5. Cut a narrow paper strip for each container and for the tube from pink paper. They should be long enough to wrap around their matching containers.
6. Draw a face on the center of each strip with a crayon or marker.
7. Tape each strip to its container, a little down from the top, Fig. b.

A. Mama Leprechaun

1. Place the end of the small container on yellow paper. Trace around it with a pencil. Draw a second circle around the traced circle to form a ring.
2. Cut out the ring. Slip it over the top of the container above the face, Fig. c. Add a paper flower.
3. Cut a red paper strip for the hair. Cut slits into one long edge and curl up. Glue the hair around the back of the face, Fig. d.
4. Cut a long strip of colored paper for a jacket. Cut a V into the center of the strip. Glue this strip below the face, Fig. e.
5. Add a paper bow to the front of the jacket.

B. Papa Leprechaun

1. Cut a green paper hat. Glue on a thin white paper band, Fig. f. Glue the hat to the large container.
2. Cut a black or white paper strip for the beard. Cut slits along one long edge and curl up. Glue the beard around the container under the face, Fig. g.
3. Cut a narrow black paper strip for a belt. Cut and glue a yellow buckle to the center of the belt. Glue the belt around the container under the beard, Fig. h.

C. Baby Leprechaun

1. Cut two small white paper triangles for a collar.
2. Glue the collar under the face on the tube, Fig. i.

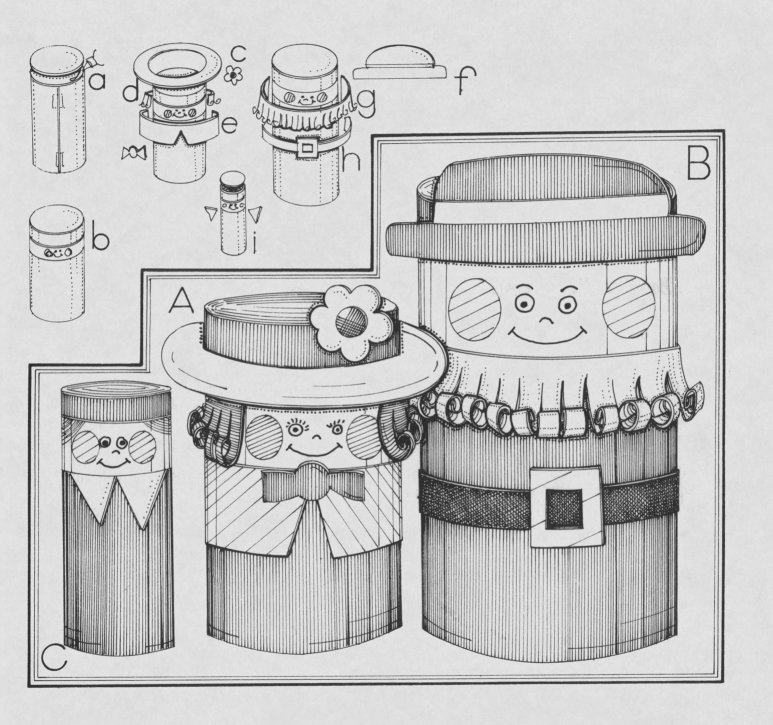

St. Bridget's Cross

An Irish lass named Bridget,
Wove crosses made of straw,
And gave these pretty woven gifts
To anyone she saw.

THINGS YOU NEED—plastic drinking straws, stapler, ribbon

A. Single-Weave Cross
1. Fold four plastic drinking straws in half. Staple the ends together, Fig. a.
2. Place a straw lengthwise in front of you.
3. Place the loop of straw 2 over the stapled end of straw 1, Fig. b.
4. Place the loop of straw 3 into the loop of straw 1, Fig. c.
5. Place the loop of straw 4 over the stapled end of straw 2, Fig. d.
6. Push the ends of straw 4 into the loop of straw 3, Fig. e.
7. Pull all four arms (stapled ends) out, forming a tight weave in the center, to form the cross, Fig. f.
8. Tie a length of ribbon in a bow around the end of each arm.

B. Double-Weave Cross (Shown in drawing)
1. Fold and staple eight straws, as described above (in Step 1).
2. Make a single-weave cross as above, using four folded straws, Fig. f.
3. Push the end of the arm on the left through the loop of straw 5, Fig. g.
4. Carefully study Figs. h, i, and j. The loops of straws 6, 7, and 8 go over the arms of the cross, working toward the right. The ends of these straws are pushed into the loops of the last straw that has been placed on the cross.
5. Pull all four arms out tightly to form a second weave of straws around the first weave, Fig. k.
6. Tie a length of ribbon into a bow around each arm.

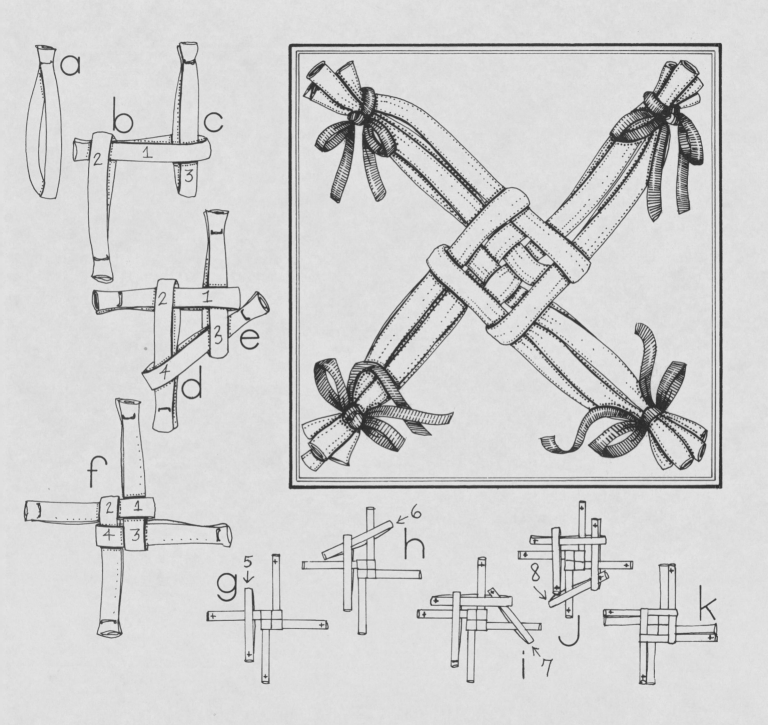

St. Patrick's Boat

A lad named Patrick, long ago,
Was kidnapped by a band
Of men who brought him in a boat,
To pretty Ireland.

THINGS YOU NEED—stapler, quart-sized milk carton, scissors, colored paper, glue, cardboard paper towel tube

1. Staple the open end of an empty quart-sized milk carton closed.
2. Cut away a side of the carton up to the peak; see shaded area in Fig. a.
3. Place the carton on brown paper. Trace around all the sides with a pencil.
4. Cut out the traced paper sides.
5. Glue or staple the paper to the sides of the carton, Fig. b. The open end faces up.
*6. Cut slits, close together, in one end of a cardboard paper towel tube, Fig. c.
7. Fold the slits outward to form tabs, Fig. d.
8. Glue the tabs to the inside of the carton at the center, Fig. e.
9. Cut a sail from colored paper. Make the top narrower than the bottom. The sides of the sail should be cut on an angle. Glue a paper P, for Patrick, on the sail.
10. Glue the sail to the tube.

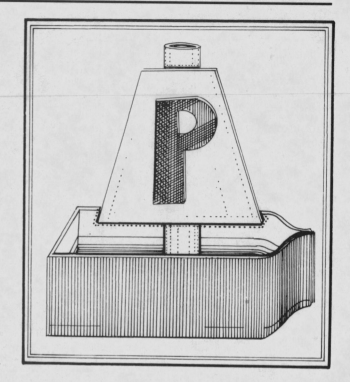

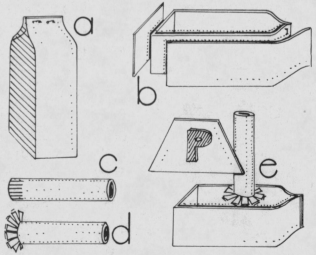

Easter Party

Easter is a springtime holiday. It is a time to decorate eggs and eagerly await the arrival of the Easter Bunny bringing a basket filled with chocolate bunnies and marshmallow chickens and eggs, all resting on a carpet of jellybeans.

Spring into action right now for an exciting Easter. This year, have a basketful of fun with an Easter party. Invite your friends to visit you and Mr. Easter Bunny himself. He will be the guest of honor among the decorated eggs, the egg cakes, and the egg puppets. The fun will continue with an old-fashioned egg hunt, and will happily end when the last jellybean has been eaten.

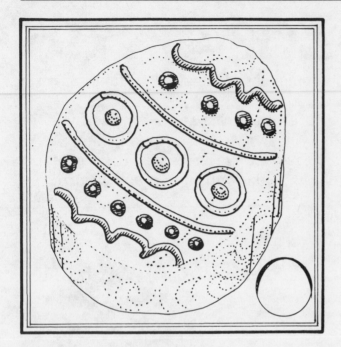

2. Cut each cake in the shape of an egg.
3. Mix the frosting according to package directions. Divide the frosting in half. Color each half with a different food coloring.
4. Frost each egg cake with a plastic knife.
5. Decorate each egg cake with designs, using gel icing in a tube.

Egg Float and Jellybean Kisses

1. Make hot chocolate and float a chocolate-covered marshmallow egg in each cup.
2. Make Easter kisses by wrapping an aluminum foil square around several jellybeans. Put them in a bowl.

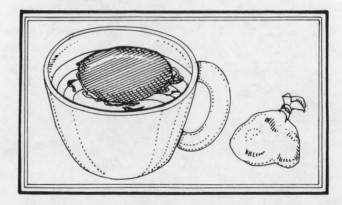

Easter Egg Cakes

A cake shaped like an Easter egg
Tastes so good to eat
That friends will want another piece
Of this party treat.

THINGS YOU NEED—cake mix, two round cake pans, plastic knife, white frosting mix, food coloring, plates, gel icing in a tube.

*1. Bake a cake in two round cake pans. Follow package directions. Remove from the pans and let cool.

Decorated Eggs

Dip hard-boiled eggs in colored dyes,
And decorate each one,
Then place them in a basket,
For Easter Party fun.

THINGS YOU NEED — hard-boiled eggs, egg or food coloring, paper towels, scissors, glue, crayons or markers

1. Color the hard-boiled eggs with egg coloring (follow package directions) or food coloring. Dry the eggs on paper towels.
2. Use your imagination in thinking up decorations. Here are some suggestions.

A. Glue rickrack around an egg.
B. Glue on print fabric hearts or designs.
C. Glue colored yarn around the eggs.
D. Glue on confetti.
E. Add lick-on stars.
F. Glue on Easter cut-outs from magazines or cards.
G. Glue on decals.
H. Write on names and designs with a crayon or marker.
I. Glue pom-pom fringe around the center of an egg.
J. Glue on small squares of colored tissue paper, overlapping each other.
K. Squeeze on glue designs. Sprinkle on glitter.
L. Glue on cake decorations.
M. Glue on dried split peas or lentils.

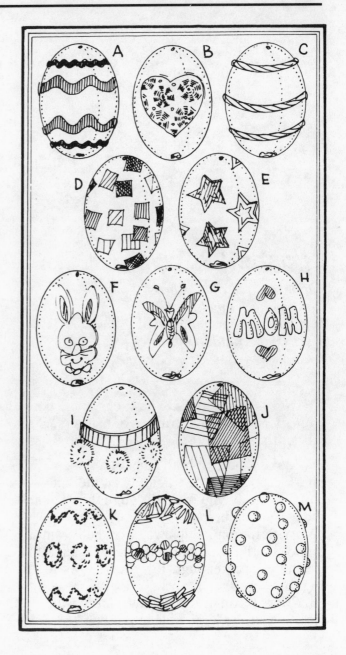

Eggshell Puppets

Puppets made of eggshells,
Don't require much.
The shell becomes the puppet's head,
A skirt's the final touch.

THINGS YOU NEED—raw egg, pin, bowl, white paper, scissors, crayons or markers, glue, fabric, thread, needle

*1. Make a hole in both ends of an egg with a pin, Fig. a. To make a hole, twist the pin back and forth until you break through the shell and the egg's membrane.

2. With the pin, chip away the shell from the pinhole in the wide end of the egg, Fig. a. Make the hole large enough for your finger to fit, Fig. b.

3. Blow through the pinhole, letting the egg flow out of the large hole into a bowl.

4. Cut two ear shapes from white paper and color the inside with a pink crayon or marker.

5. Glue the ears to the end of the egg that has the pinhole, Fig. c.

6. Draw a face on the egg with a crayon or marker, Fig. d.

7. Cut a long piece of fabric for a skirt.

*8. Thread a needle and knot the end of the thread.

*9. Move the needle in and out of the fabric along one long edge, Fig. e.

10. Remove the needle. Bring both ends of the thread together, Fig. f.

11. Gather the fabric, and tie the ends of the thread in a bow, Fig. g. Your finger should fit through the gathered end.

12. To work the puppet, place the fabric over your hand and push one finger through the gathered end. Place the egg head on your finger, Fig. h.

13. Make a bear, raccoon, deer, or any other animal for a puppet show.

Mr. Easter Bunny Centerpiece

An animal cuddly and cute
Has an Easter delivery route.
He's a really big giver,
Dyed eggs he'll deliver,
Plus candy and trinkets to boot.

THINGS YOU NEED—white paper, pencil, ruler, scissors, colored paper, glue, crayons or markers

1. Divide a sheet of white paper into four equal parts with a small fifth section at one end, as shown in Fig. a. Use a pencil and ruler.

2. Draw a line across the center of the paper; see dotted line in Fig. b.

3. Draw a curved line from the outer top corners of sections 2 and 3 to the dotted line, as shown in Fig. b. These are the ears.

4. Cut away the paper above the dotted line and around the curved ears, Fig. c.

5. Fold along the drawn line between the ears; see sections 2 and 3 in Fig. d.

6. Cut a nose into the folded edge. The first cut goes up from the fold towards the ears. The second cut goes up towards the fold but not into it; see top arrow in Fig. d. Do not cut the nose off.

7. Cut a small down slit below the nose near the bottom edge; see bottom arrow in Fig. d.

8. Open the paper. Make the bunny's face with colored paper cut-outs and a marker or crayon, Fig. e.

9. Fold the paper along all drawn lines to form a box. Glue the small section (section 5) to the outside, Fig. f.

10. Pull out the cut nose.

11. Cut a bow tie from colored paper and decorate with polka dots. Slip it into the slit below the nose; see arrow in Fig. g.

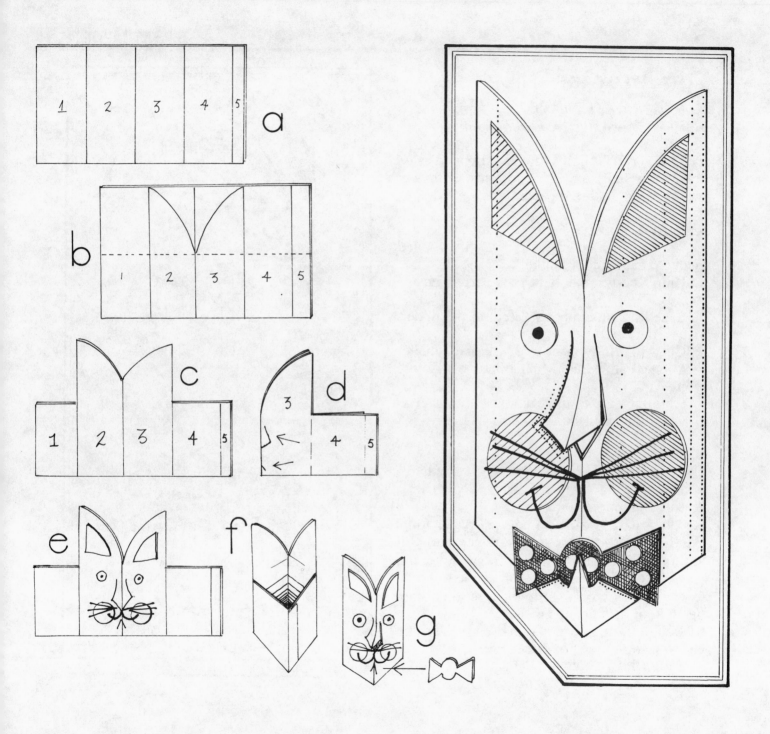

Egg Bunnies

What is Easter with no bunny!
Make these two, they're kind of funny.

THINGS YOU NEED—two hard-boiled eggs, crayons or markers, glue, cotton ball, macaroni, scissors, colored paper, tape

A. Billy Bunny

1. Draw a face on the wide end of a hard-boiled egg with a crayon or marker.
2. Glue a cotton ball tail to the narrow end of the egg.
3. Glue four tube macaroni feet to the underside of the egg.
4. Cut two white paper ears. Cut two smaller pink inner ears. Glue the pink inner ears to the white ears.
5. Glue the ears to the egg above the face, as shown in the drawing.

B. Betty Bunny

1. Draw a face near the narrow end of a hard-boiled egg with a crayon or marker.
2. Cut and glue ears to the egg.
3. Cut a narrow strip of colored paper for a skirt. Tape around the middle of the egg.
4. Cut off the ends of a cotton swab for the paws. Glue in place at the top of the skirt.
5. Cut a very narrow strip of paper and draw two feet in the center, Fig. a.
6. Roll the strip into a ring small enough for the egg to rest on. Tape in place, Fig. b.
7. Stand Betty Bunny in the ring.

Halloween Party

Halloween is the yearly celebration for all ghosts and goblins, witches and ghouls. It is the one day a year to be the scary creature of your choice. The streets are filled with creatures knocking on doors and trick-or-treating.

A costume party should be the meeting place for happy monsters to catch their breath. So invite all of the friendly neighborhood creatures to your haunted home. Serve a cake shaped like a pumpkin, and a special witches' potion, and play Halloween games. Have fun, because at midnight the magic spell of Halloween ends.

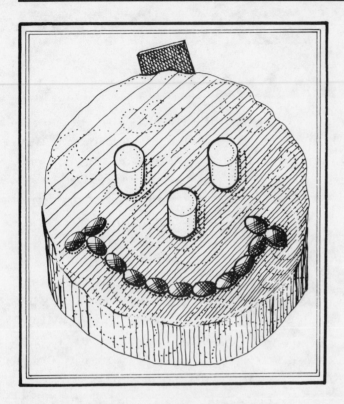

*1. Bake a cake in a large round cake pan (or bake two cakes in smaller round pans). Follow package directions. Remove and let cool.

2. Place the cake on a large plate.

3. Mix the frosting according to package directions. Add yellow and a little red food coloring to make it orange colored.

4. Frost the cake with a plastic knife.

5. Make a face with marshmallow eyes and nose and a jellybean mouth.

6. Cut a rectangle from brown paper and push it into the side of the cake at the top for a stem.

Pumpkin Cakes

After trick-or-treating,
As a ghoul or beast,
Invite your friends to join you,
At a party feast.

THINGS YOU NEED—orange cake mix, round cake pan, plate, white frosting mix, food coloring, plastic knife, marshmallows, black jelly beans, scissors, brown paper

Orange Juice Sparkle

Orange juice is the color of pumpkins and makes a great drink for Halloween. Add some club soda to give it a sparkle and a sprinkle of cinnamon for extra flavor.

A Cackling Witch's Hat

Witches hats are pointy,
With brims so very wide,
Each guest should get a special hat,
'Cause candy's stuffed inside.

THINGS YOU NEED—black and white paper, scissors, tape, pencil, candies, glue

1. Roll a piece of black paper into a cone and tape in place, Fig. a.
2. Trim the bottom edge to form a circle, Fig. b.
3. Cut short slits into the bottom edge of the cone, Fig. b.
4. Fold the slit edge toward the inside of the cone to form tabs, Fig. c.
5. Place the cone on a piece of black paper. Draw a circle a little away from the bottom of the cone, Fig. d.
6. Cut out the circle.
7. Place candies inside the cone.
8. Squeeze glue on the tabs, Fig. e. Press the circle on the glued tabs. Let dry standing up.
9. Cut a thin white strip of paper, Fig. f. Glue it around the bottom of the cone and tape in place.

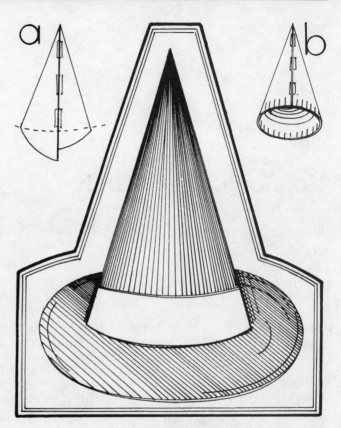

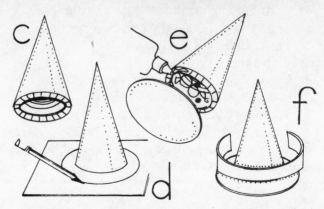

Not-So-Wicked Witch

Here is a young witch named Jean,
Who many think wicked and mean,
But she's really quite good,
Only misunderstood —
So invite her for next Halloween.

THINGS YOU NEED—scissors, colored paper, round cardboard container (from salt, oatmeal, etc.), tape, pencil, glue, paper cup, crayons or markers, paper punch

1. Cut a piece of black paper as high as the round container. It should be long enough to wrap around the container plus a little extra.
2. Tape the paper to the container, Fig. a.
3. Place one end of the container on black paper and trace around it.
4. Cut out the traced circle. Glue it to the top of the container, Fig. a.
5. Wrap a paper cup in a skin-colored paper, Fig. b. Tape in place, Fig. c.
6. Trim away the paper at the top and bottom edges of the cup, Fig. d.

7. Draw a face on the front of the cup with a crayon or marker, Fig. e.
8. Wrap a piece of black paper into a cone large enough to fit over the small end of the cup. Tape, and trim the bottom edge to form a circle. Place it on the cup, Fig. f.
9. Cut a black paper ring to fit over the cone, Fig. g. It should fall near the bottom edge of the cone.
10. Cut a long and narrow strip of white paper.
11. Fold the paper evenly back and forth in small folds, Fig. h. Use up all the paper.
12. Open up the folded paper. Punch a hole in the top of each folded section with a paper punch, Fig. i.
13. Weave a length of yarn in and out of the holes to make a collar, Fig. j.
14. Make two arms from black paper. Cut out two hands from skin-colored paper. Attach to the arms, Fig. k.
15. Cut a broom shape from yellow paper. Glue it to a brown paper handle, Fig. l.
16. Tie the collar around the head, Fig. m. Glue the arms to the sides of the container, Fig. n. Glue the broom to one hand.

a b c d

e f g

h

i

J

k

l

m

n

Pumpkin Creations

Pumpkins grow in different shapes,
Skinny, fat, and tall.
Turn some into dogs and apes
And a coach for a royal ball

A. Witch Pumpkin
1. Roll a sheet of black paper into a cone and tape in place. Trim the bottom edge to form a circle.
2. Draw a face on the pumpkin with a marker. Glue on yarn hair.
3. Put the cone hat on top of the pumpkin.

B. Pumpkin Vase
*1. Cut away the top of a pumpkin, making a zigzag design. Clean out the seeds.
2. Place a small branch with autumn leaves inside the pumpkin.

C. Pumpkin Centerpiece
*1. Cut away the top of a pumpkin for a lid. Clean out the seeds.
2. Wrap little gifts. Tie a long piece of ribbon to each gift.
3. Place the ends of the ribbons inside the pumpkin. Replace the lid.

D. Pumpkin Toss Game
*1. Cut away the tops of three small pumpkins. Clean out the seeds.
2. Paint a different number on each pumpkin.
3. Toss Ping-Pong balls at the pumpkins, trying to get them into the hole. Add up each player's score by totaling the numbers on the pumpkins that the Ping-Pong balls land in.

E. Pin the Nose on the Pumpkin
1. Paint eyes, an X for a nose, and a big smile on a pumpkin.
2. Cut out many paper triangles. Stick double-sided tape to the back of each triangle.
3. Blindfold each player. The player who sticks the nose closest to the X wins.

F. Lacy Pumpkin
*1. Cut away the top of a pumpkin for a lid. Clean out the seeds.
*2. Make a face and a hat design, on the lid, by pushing a sharp pencil completely through the pumpkin.
*3. Place a candle inside, light it, and replace the lid.

G. Cinderella's Carriage
1. Cut colored paper wheels, a door, and a strip of paper for the front seat.
2. Attach the paper cut-outs to the pumpkin with toothpicks.

H. Pumpkin Animals
1. Cut out paper ears and attach to a pumpkin with toothpicks.
2. Add on eyes, nose, and mouth with a marker or poster paint.

I. Pumpkin House
Draw a house on a pumpkin with a marker.

Escape the Ghost Game

Pretend you're running from a ghost,
One dark and scary night.
This candy trail will lead you home,
Far from the ghoulish sight.

THINGS YOU NEED—orange and black jellybeans, scissors, red paper, plastic bottle caps, dice

1. Cut an arrow from red paper. Place it on one side of a table.

2. Make a path of orange jellybeans, leading from the arrow and winding back to it. Every so often replace an orange jellybean with a black one.

3. To play the game, each player gets a plastic bottle cap. In turn, each player rolls a die. He or she jumps the number of jellybeans corresponding to the number on the die. If he or she lands on a black jellybean, he or she must go back two beans. The first to complete the trail to the arrow wins.

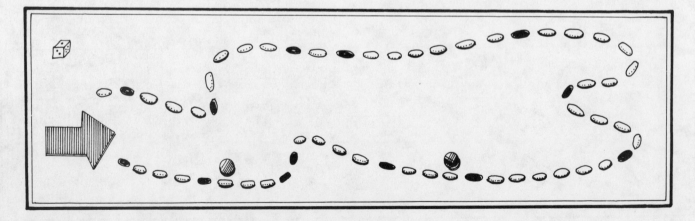

Thanksgiving Party

The Pilgrims came to America in 1620. They named their little settlement Plymouth. A year later they held a great celebration. It was harvest time, and the settlers were thankful to have survived the harsh first year in their new country. The Indians were the guests of honor at this three-day feast. All dined on fish, wild fruits, vegetables, corn bread, and, of course, wild turkey.

This first Thanksgiving celebration happened over three hundred years ago. Today it is a popular holiday. Add your contributions to this year's Thanksgiving party. Bake a cake in the shape of the *Mayflower*, the Pilgrims' ship. Give everyone a Pilgrim's hat and scatter turkey and Indian corn decorations around your home. Discover how much fun Thanksgiving can really be.

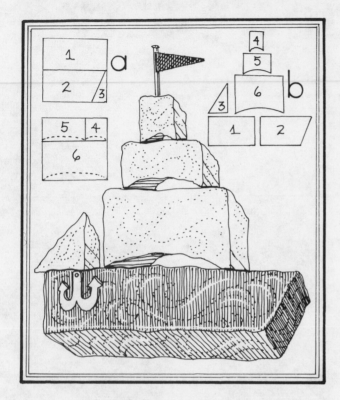

Mayflower Cake

The Pilgrims sailed from England,
On a long and lonely trip,
Arriving in a strange, new land,
The Mayflower *was their ship.*

THINGS YOU NEED — cake mix, two square cake pans, plastic knife, cookie sheet, aluminum foil, white and chocolate frosting mixes, scissors, glue, paper, plastic drinking straw

*1. Bake a cake in two square pans. Follow package directions. Remove from the pans and let cool.
2. Cut each cake carefully, Fig. a.
3. Cover a cookie sheet with aluminum foil.
4. Arrange the cut cakes on the cookie sheet, as shown in Fig. b. All pieces should be touching each other.
5. Mix the frosting according to package directions. Frost the ship with chocolate frosting and the sails with the white frosting. Use a plastic knife.
6. Cut a paper anchor shape and stick it on the side of the ship.
7. Cut a triangle flag and glue it to one end of half of a drinking straw.
8. Push the other end into the top sail.

Pilgrim Pies and Drinks

If you don't have time to make the Mayflower cake, why not serve a pie? Pie is an American food so at Thanksgiving serve your favorite fruit-flavored variety. Mix apple and cranberry juices with ginger ale and add a scoop of vanilla ice cream for a delicious treat.

Plymouth Rock Game

Start in England with your ship,
The wind is strongly blowing.
Roll the dice and start the trip,
America's where you're going.

THINGS YOU NEED—large sheet of paper, crayons or markers, rock, play clay, walnut shells or plastic bottle caps, colored paper, glue, toothpicks, rock, dice

1. Color a quarter of a circle on two opposite corners of a large sheet of paper with a crayon or marker.
2. Write the word, "England," around one quarter-circle and the word, "America," around the other.
3. Draw a continuous wavy line going every which way from "England" to "America."
4. Place a small ball of play clay inside a walnut shell or plastic bottle cap.
5. Cut a colored paper triangle. Glue it to one end of a toothpick to make a flag.
6. Push the toothpick into the clay to form a ship. Make several ships with flags.
7. Lay the paper on the floor. Put a rock on the American quarter-circle.
8. To play the game, each player gets a ship. Everyone starts in England. One person at a time rolls a pair of dice and jumps from wave peak to wave peak. The number of waves depends on the total number on the dice. The first person to reach America wins.

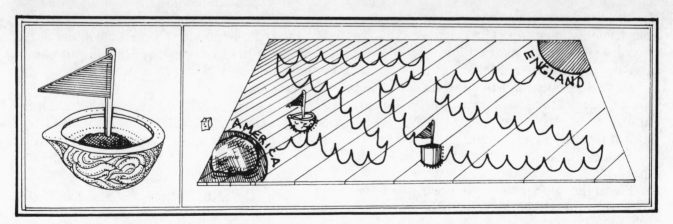

Turkey Centerpiece

A bird that is thought of as perky
And hobbles and wobbles quite jerky,
Is known to us all,
Gobble, gobble, its call,
It's your old friend the Thanksgiving turkey.

THINGS YOU NEED—poster paints, kitchen cleanser, brush, paper cup, plastic tub (butter, cottage cheese, etc.), colored paper, pencil, scissors, glue, lightweight cardboard, crayons or markers

1. Mix brown poster paint with a little kitchen cleanser in a paper cup. The cleanser will help the paint stick to the plastic tub.
2. Paint a plastic tub, Fig. a. Let dry.
3. Place the open end of the plastic tub on brown paper. Trace around it with a pencil, Fig. b.
4. Cut out the traced circle.
5. Squeeze glue around the edge of the circle, Fig. c.
6. Press the glued circle to the rim of the plastic tub, Fig. d. Let dry.

*7. Cut a small, vertical slit into the tub a little below the smaller rim, Fig. e.
*8. Turn the tub around and cut another slit, this time horizontal, a little below the smaller rim, Fig. f, opposite the first slit.
9. Cut a long, narrow cardboard rectangle for the head. Cut another rectangle, a little shorter and wider than the first, for the legs.
10. Draw the turkey's head and legs on the rectangles, similar to the ones shown in the drawing, with a crayon or a marker, Fig. g. Cut out.
11. Paint the head red and the legs yellow. Draw eyes and a beak on the head.
12. Push the head into the vertical slit, Fig. h. Push the pointed end of the legs into the horizontal slit, Fig. i. Squeeze a little glue along the slits and let dry.
13. Cut paper feathers of different sizes. Draw a feather design on each with a crayon, Fig. j.
14. Glue the feathers to the wide end of the tub, Fig. j. Place largest feathers by the head and the smallest by the feet.
15. Glue a paper wing shape to each side of the tub. Glue two red circles under the beak.

Indian Corn Decorations

The Indians brought a special treat,
That first Thanksgiving morn,
A tasty gift so good to eat,
A bunch of Indian corn.

THINGS YOU NEED—long balloons, newspaper, white glue, paper cups, waxed paper, brush, white poster paint, food coloring, scissors, green paper, pencil, string

1. Blow up two balloons and knot the necks, Fig. a.
2. Tear newspaper into short, narrow strips.
3. Pour glue into a paper cup. Thin by mixing in a little water.
4. Place a strip of newspaper on a sheet of waxed paper. Brush one side of the strip with glue, Fig. b.
5. Place the glued side of the strip on a balloon. Continue gluing and adding strips, covering the entire balloon, Fig. c. Cover both balloons with two layers of strips.
6. Let balloons dry overnight.
7. Paint the balloon with white poster paint, Fig. d.
8. Mix yellow food coloring and glue in a paper cup, Fig. e.
9. Paint the balloons with the glue paint, Fig. f. Place on waxed paper and let dry.
10. Mix different food colorings in small amounts of glue. Paint scattered corn kernels on both balloons, Fig. g. Let dry.
11. Cut a large green rectangle. Fold it evenly back and forth, using up all the paper, Fig. h.
12. Draw a leaf shape on the front of the paper, as shown in the drawing, Fig. i.
13. Cut out the leaf through all layers. Leave uncut some paper on both sides at the bottom.
14. Place one end of the cut leaves around the neck of a balloon, Fig. j.
15. Roll the remaining leaves around the neck.
16. Tie the leaves around the stem with string, Fig. k. Leave one end of the string long for hanging. Make several Indian corn balloons.

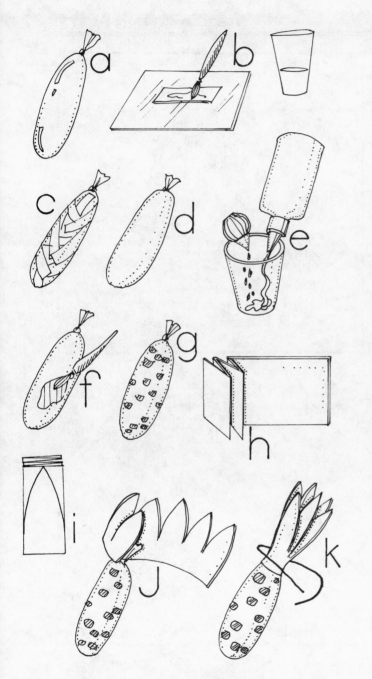

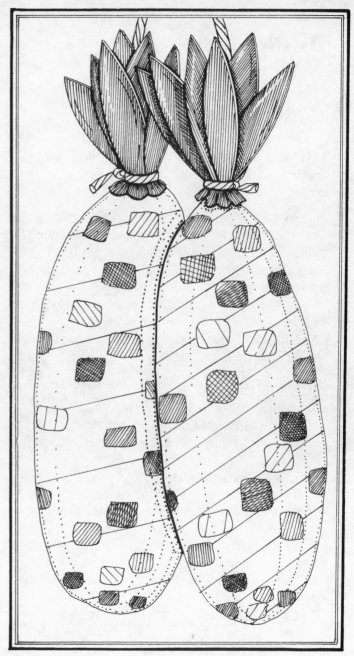

Pilgrim's Hat

It's shaped like a cone,
But the top is flat.
Can you guess what it is?
It's a Pilgrim's hat.

THINGS YOU NEED—black, white, and yellow paper, tape, scissors, glue, light-colored crayon

1. Roll a large sheet of black paper into a cone. You may have to tape two sheets together to make a cone large enough. The opening at the bottom should be wider than at the top. Tape in place, Fig. a.
2. Trim the top and bottom edges of the cone, Fig. b.
3. Cut short slits, close together, into the top and bottom rims of the cone, Fig. c.
4. Place the larger end of the cone on a large sheet of black paper.
5. Trace around it with a light crayon (so you can see the mark). Draw a second circle a few inches away from the traced circle to form a ring, Fig. d.
6. Cut out the ring for the hat's brim.
7. Fold the smaller slit edge of the hat toward the inside to form tabs, Fig. e. Fold the larger slit edge toward the outside to form tabs, Fig f.
8. Cut a circle to fit over the top of the cone. Glue it to the tabs, Fig. g.
9. Slip the brim over the cone and glue the bottom tabs, Fig. h.
10. Cut a thin white strip of paper. Glue it around the hat near the brim. Glue a yellow buckle shape to the front of the band.

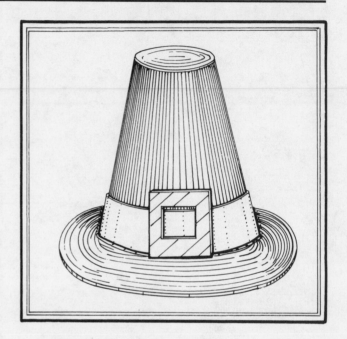

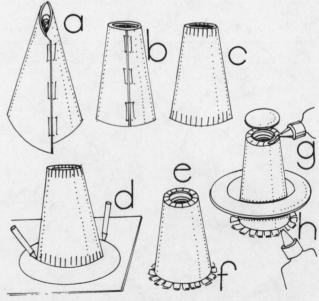

Chanukah Party

Chanukah is a very happy holiday for the Jewish people. Two thousand years ago their ancestors were trapped by Antiochus IV who wanted to force them to pray to other gods. They had only one day's supply of oil left yet miraculously their lamp burned in the temple for eight days. There was much rejoicing at such a wondrous sight. Today, Chanukah is celebrated over eight days. Delicious foods are eaten, gifts are given, and the dreidel game is played.

Set aside one of the eight days of Chanukah to have a party. Make sure the candle for this day is burning brightly in your menorah — a candlestick with eight branches used to represent the oil lamp from many years ago. Serve every guest a piece of the dreidel cake. Hang the Star of David for all to see. Don't forget to spin the dreidel and play other games. This will be the brightest of all the days of Chanukah.

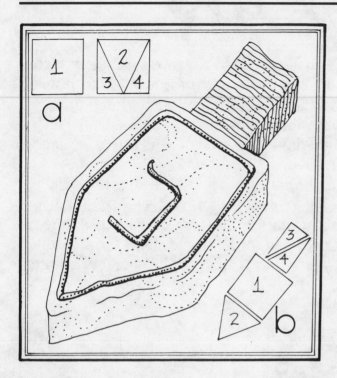

Dreidel Cake

Eyes will shine, make no mistake,
When you serve this dreidel cake.

THINGS YOU NEED—cake mix, two square cake pans, plastic knife, cookie sheet, aluminum foil, white frosting mix, food coloring, blue gel icing in a tube

*1. Bake a cake in two square cake pans. Follow package directions. Remove from the pans and let cool.

2. Leave one cake uncut and cut the other, as shown in the drawing, Fig. a.

3. Cover a cookie sheet with aluminum foil.

4. Arrange the cut cake around the uncut cake, as shown in Fig. b. All pieces should be touching.

5. Mix the frosting according to package directions. Add blue food coloring to one-quarter of the white frosting.

6. Spread blue frosting on the handle of the dreidel with a plastic knife. Frost the remaining cake with white frosting.

7. Decorate with blue gel icing, as shown in the drawing.

Milk and Honey

For sweet treats with a special taste, spoon honey mixed with strawberry preserves on top of a brick of vanilla ice cream. You can also stir the honey-strawberry mixture in cold milk.

Make an Israeli flag by drawing a Star of David and two blue stripes on a strip of white paper (see the illustration). Fold the strip around a toothpick and glue it together. Stick it in the brick of vanilla ice cream.

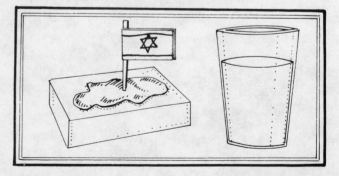

Dreidel Game

Place the dreidel in one hand
And give it a good spin.
If you're lucky it will land
On Gimel, and you'll win.

THINGS YOU NEED—cardboard, scissors, crayons or markers, short sharp pencil, colored paper

*1. Cut a small square from cardboard with scissors.

2. With a crayon or marker, draw a line from one corner to the opposite corners, dividing the square into four equal, triangle-shaped sections, Fig. a.

3. Draw symbols in each section as shown in Fig. b.

4. Carefully twist a short pencil into the center of the square, where the lines cross, Fig. c.

5. Cut paper circles for coins. Write 1¢ on each circle.

6. To play the game, each player first puts a paper penny in the game. Each player then spins the dreidel by spinning the eraser end of the pencil. If the dreidel lands on Nun (1), the player gets nothing; Shin (2), the player has to put one penny in the pot; Hay (3), the player takes half of the pennies in the pot; and Gimel (4), the player takes all the pennies.

7. If you substitute popcorn for the pennies, winners can win a tasty snack.

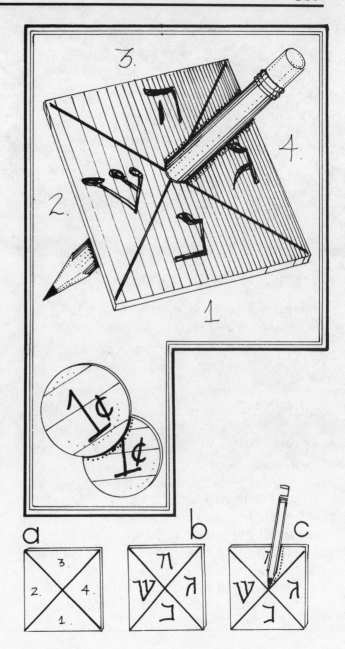

Candle Menorah

Chanukah is eight days long,
And every holiday night,
Add another candle flame,
To the growing light.

THINGS YOU NEED—colored paper, pencil, ruler, scissors, tape or glue

1. Divide a long piece of colored paper into four sections with a pencil and ruler. The first two (the largest) are the same size; see 1 in Fig. a. The third section is half the size of the first; see 2 in Fig. a. The fourth section is half the size of the third; see 3 in Fig. a.

2. Fold the first section over the second, along the drawn line, Fig. b.

3. Draw eighteen lines, equally spaced, across the paper, Fig. c. Start at the fold and go halfway down the paper.

4. Cut along the lines, forming bars.

5. Fold the paper along the two remaining drawn lines, Fig. d.

6. Fold the paper into a triangle, with the smallest section tucked inside, Fig. e. Tape or glue in place.

7. Fold the bars on both sides of the middle bar (that is the ninth and eleventh bars) down into the triangle; see shaded areas in Fig. e. This remaining middle bar, or candle, is called the shamos candle and in a real menorah it is used to light the others.

8. Fold the first and third bars down, leaving the second bar standing. This is the first candle for the first day of Chanukah.

9. Cut flame shapes from red paper. Glue or tape one to the top of the first candle and one to the shamos candle.

10. Every day of Chanukah, fold down every other bar to form a new candle. Light each new candle with a paper flame.

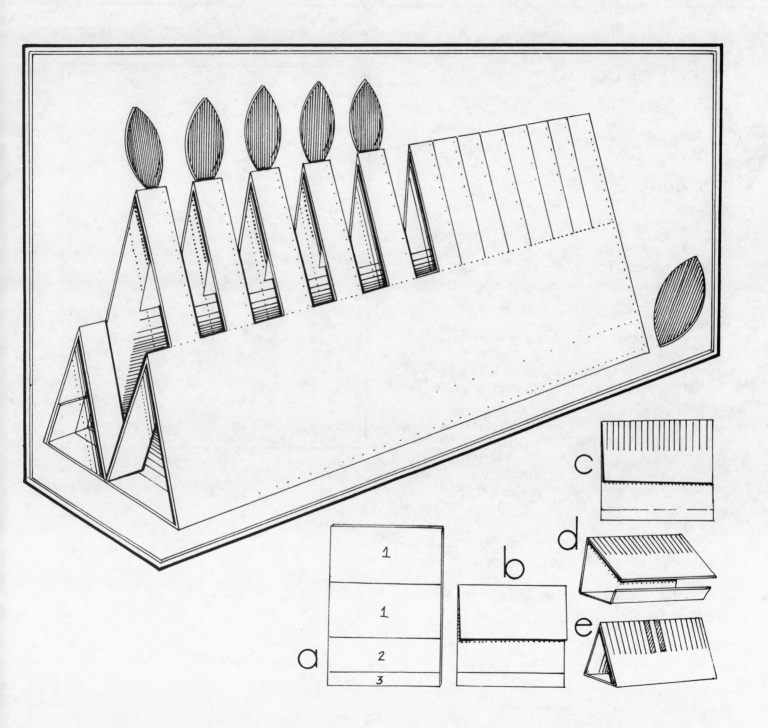

a

1

1

2

3

b

c

d

e

Star of David

The Star of David symbolizes
Jews from near and far.
For your Chanukah party,
Make this six-point star.

THINGS YOU NEED — scissors, colored paper, ruler, pencil, glue or tape, paper punch, string

1. Cut twelve very long, narrow strips of colored paper, all the same size.
2. Mark off a small section at one end of each strip with a pencil; see X in Fig. a. This will be the tab.
3. Divide the remaining strip into three equal sections. Use a pencil and ruler, Fig. a.
4. Fold along all drawn lines of a strip. Fold the tab in to form a triangle, and glue or tape in place, Fig. b.
5. Fold and glue all the strips into triangles.
6. Glue three triangles together, side by side, to form a row, Fig. c. Make a second row.
7. Glue the two rows together, as shown in Fig. c. You will have a six-sided shape.
8. Glue a triangle to each side of the shape, Fig. d.
9. Punch two holes, one opposite the other, through the point of one triangle with a paper punch.
10. Knot a length of string into the punched hole. Hang the star.

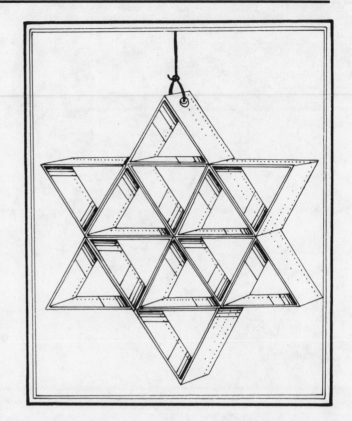

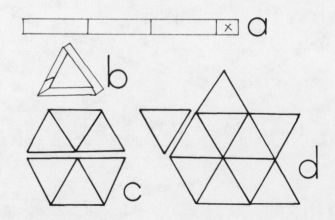

Deck The Halls Christmas Party

Christmas is a magical holiday. It is as if someone waved a fairy wand over the Earth, and it touched everyone. People you meet seem friendlier. Cold, dark days become bright and warm with Christmas decorations and colored lights everywhere you look. The best treat of all is waking up on Christmas morning to find presents under the tree.

Santa Claus is always busy so why not be his helper this year. Spread a little happiness by inviting your friends to a Christmas party. Brighten your home with hand-made decorations and a wreath on the door. Invite your friends in for food and glug. Don't forget to save a little food for Santa. He will be hungry when he arrives with your gifts.

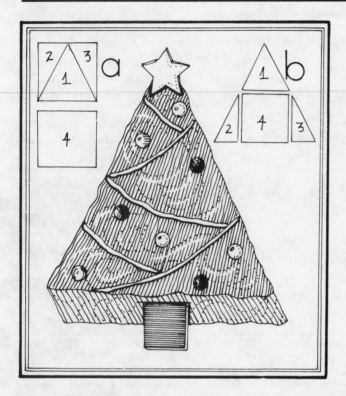

Tannenbaum Cake

This cake, shaped like a Christmas tree,
Tastes delicious – you'll soon see.

THINGS YOU NEED—cake mix, two square cake pans, plastic knife, cookie sheet, aluminum foil, white frosting mix, food coloring, gel icing in a tube, round candies, colored paper, scissors

*1. Bake a cake in two square cake pans. Follow package directions. Remove from the pans and let cool.

2. Cut one cake, as shown in the drawing, Fig. a.

3. Cover a cookie sheet with aluminum foil.

4. Arrange the cut and uncut cake on the cookie sheet, as shown in Fig. b. All sides should be touching.

5. Mix the frosting according to package directions. Add green food coloring.

6. Spread the frosting evenly over the entire cake with a plastic knife.

7. Make a Christmas garland with gel icing in a tube and decorate with round candies.

8. Cut a yellow paper star and a brown paper tree trunk.

9. Push the trunk in the center of the bottom of the cake. Place the star at the point.

Glug

Make a warm holiday drink by slightly heating equal amounts of of grape juice and red fruit punch. Add raisins and slivered almonds to the warm drink.

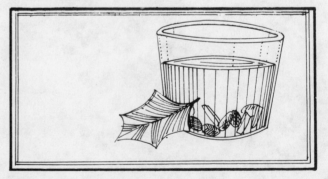

Handmade Greeting Cards

It's certainly more special,
To send a handmade card.
So make some for the ones you love,
It isn't very hard.

THINGS YOU NEED — scissors, white or colored paper, cardboard, pencil, poster paint, brush, envelopes

1. Cut folded white or colored paper to fit inside an envelope.
2. Cut small pieces of cardboard, the size you wish your letters to be, to spell the word, "Noel" (which means Christmas).

3. Draw a letter in block form on each piece of cardboard, Fig. a.
4. Cut out the letters, Fig. b.
5. Glue each letter *backwards* on a slightly larger square of cardboard, Fig. c.
6. Paint the letter with poster paint, Fig. d. Be careful not to get paint on the background cardboard.
7. Place the painted letter on the front of the folded paper at the left near the folded edge. Press hard but don't move the cardboard, Fig. e.
8. Print the letters, N, O, E, L, in order.
9. Cut holly leaves and circle berries from cardboard. Make printers, just as you did for the letters. Print the holly and berries under the letters.

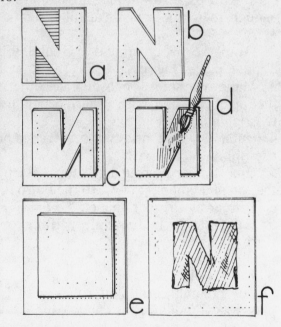

Jolly Holiday Decorations

As party decorations,
These will nicely do.
Candy canes and reindeer,
And hanging candles, too.

THINGS YOU NEED—scissors, white and colored paper, cardboard tubes (bathroom tissue and paper towel), tape, pencil, glue, string, crayons or markers, round cardboard container (salt, oatmeal, etc.), paper punch

A. Candy Cane

1. Cut a piece of white paper as high as a cardboard paper towel tube. It should be long enough to wrap around the tube plus a little extra.
2. Wrap the paper around the tube, Fig. a. Tape in place, Fig. b.
*3. Make two holes, opposite each other, near the top of the tube, with a sharp pencil, using a twisting motion, Fig. c.
4. Cut a very long, narrow strip of red paper, or use ribbon, if you wish.
5. Glue the strip around the tube, starting at the top and coiling it down to the bottom, Fig. d. Trim away the extra paper.
6. Knot string in the holes. Hang on the Christmas tree.

B. Reindeer

1. Cover small cardboard tubes with brown paper, as you did for the candy cane.

2. Cut two paper antlers for each tube. Cut circles for eyes, noses, and jingle-bell collars.
3. Glue the cut-outs to the tubes.
4. Draw on a mouth, and make small crosses on the bells with a crayon or marker.

C. Yule Log

1. Cover a round cardboard container with brown paper, as above.
2. Place one end of the container on brown paper. Trace around the end with a pencil.
3. Cut out the traced circles and glue them to each end.
4. Cover a tube with white paper. Cut a flame shape from red paper. Glue it to the inside of the tube at one end.
5. Tape the candle in the center of the container.
6. Cut green paper holly leaves and red circle berries.
7. Glue the leaves and berries to the front of the yule log.

D. Hanging Candle

1. Make a candle, holly leaves, and berries, as described in the Yule Log.
2. Glue the leaves and berries to the bottom end of the candle, at the front.
3. Cut a yellow paper circle. Glue it to the back of the candle, behind the flame.
4. Punch a hole near the top of the circle with a paper punch. Knot string in the hole for hanging.

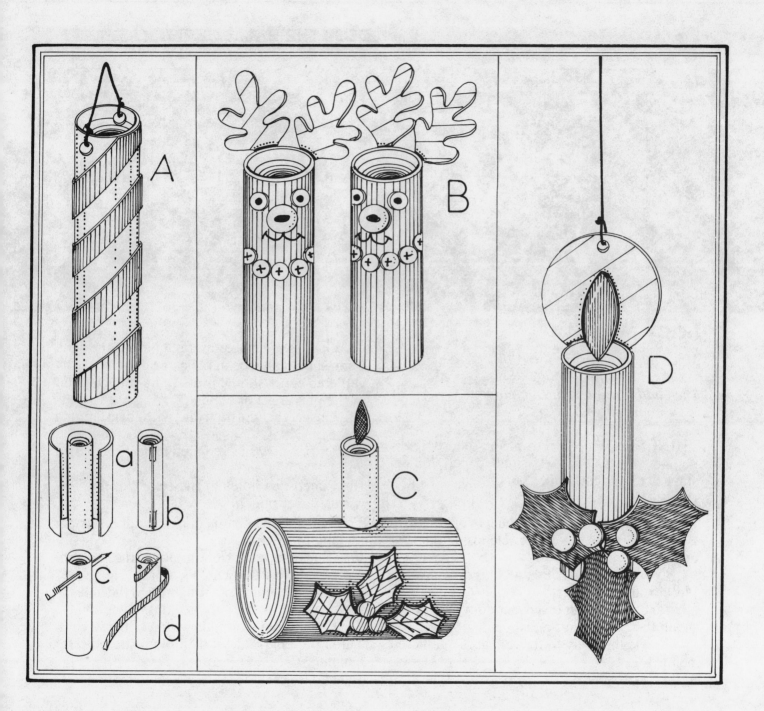

Lacy Wreath

Make a lacy Christmas wreath
It's not a lengthy chore.
Then add a string so it can hang —
A welcome on your door.

THINGS YOU NEED—poster board (oak-tag), compass, scissors, small paper doilies, stapler, red paper, paper punch, glue or tape, yarn

1. Draw a large circle on a sheet of oaktag with a compass. Draw another circle inside the first circle to form a ring.

2. Cut out the ring, Fig. a. This includes the piece from the center.

3. Pinch the center of a paper doily and gather up all the edges, Fig. b.

4. Staple the doily to the ring at the gathered point, Fig. c.

5. Gather and staple more doilies to the ring. They should all face in the same direction. The gathered edges should overlap the stapled point of the previous doily, Fig. d.

6. Cover the entire ring with overlapping doilies.

7. Draw a bow shape on red paper, Fig. e. Cut out.

8. Punch two holes in the center of the bow with a paper punch.

9. Cut ribbon ends from two small red paper rectangles, Fig. f.

10. Glue or tape the ribbon ends to the center of the bow, below the punched holes, Fig. g.

11. Extend a length of yarn through the holes of the bow, Fig. h. Tie the bow to the wreath.

12. Punch a hole through the top of the wreath. Thread a length of yarn through the hole for hanging.

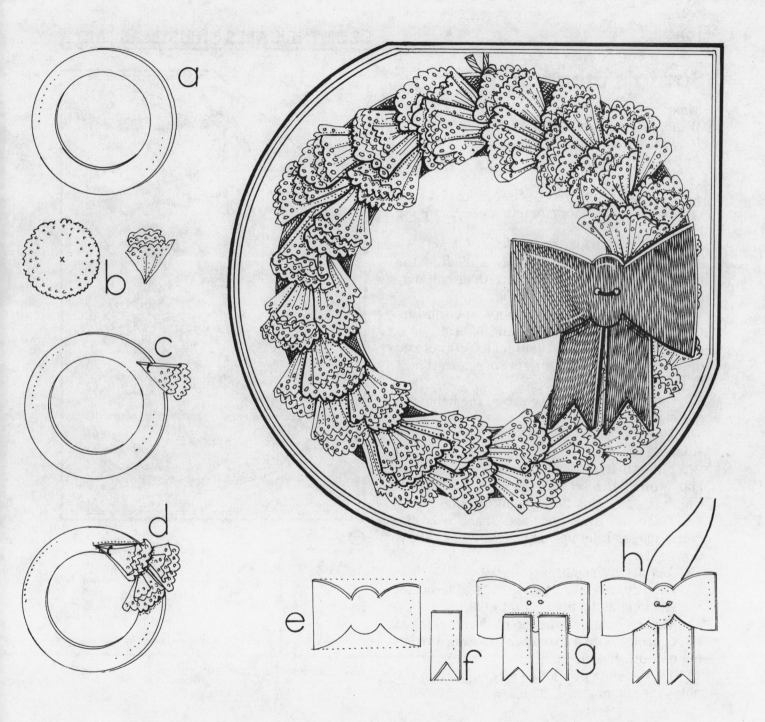

Santa's Stocking

Make a pretty stocking
Which takes no special trick.
It will be filled at Christmas
By jolly old St. Nick.

THINGS YOU NEED—scissors, paper, pencil, ruler, colored fabric or felt, glue, pom-pom, cord

1. Cut a large paper rectangle.
2. With a pencil and ruler, draw a line from the top to the bottom, a little more than half way from the left edge; see X in Fig. a.
3. Draw a line across the paper, one-third up from the bottom edge; see Z in Fig. a.
4. Draw a curve on the bottom left corner and draw a point at the lower right corner, as shown in Fig. a.
5. Cut out the stocking pattern; see light area in Fig. a.
6. Use this pattern to cut two fabric or felt stocking shapes.
7. Squeeze a thick line of glue down the sides and around the bottom (foot) of one shape, Fig. b. Do not glue the straight top edge.
8. Place the other stocking shape over the glued shape. Line up the edges, Fig. c. Press down, flat.
9. Let dry overnight.
10. Glue a green fabric tree shape to one side of the stocking and a pom-pom to the toe.
*11. Make a hole into the top of the stocking at both corners with a sharp pencil, using a twisting motion, Fig. d.
12. Tie the ends of a long piece of cord in the holes for hanging.

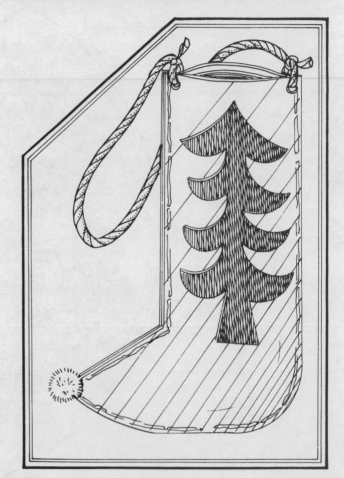

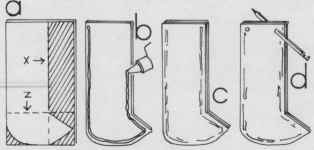

Soap Snow People

Although this pair is made from soap,
Not really snow at all,
They look like Frosty and his wife,
Who've come to pay a call.

–Ivory® soap, tracing
knife, paper, beads or
corns, glue

bar of Ivory® soap.
cing paper under the
the soap on the paper.
on a larger circle, as

Rub the side of a pen-
circles, Fig. b.
of the drawing on the
outline.
draw along the cir-
c. Press hard on the
per.
see the transferred
the soap, Fig. d.
ap around the lines
and f.

corners to make a

whole peppercorns
ons, and necklace.

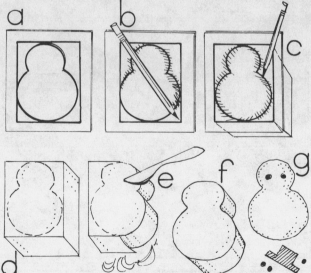

Paper Plate Angel

A pretty Christmas angel,
For your table or your tree,
Is really not too hard to make,
For all your friends to see.

THINGS YOU NEED—pencil, paper plate
with a scalloped edge, scissors, paper clip, yellow paper, glue, crayons or markers

1. Draw a line across the center of a paper plate
with a pencil.
2. Draw a head and neck, and two arms centered on the line, as shown in Fig. a. Make the
arms and head separate, do not attach.
3. Cut through the center line on both sides of
the plate up to and underneath the arms. Continue to cut out along the top of the arms only.
Stop at the shoulders, leaving them attached.
4. Poke one point of a scissors into the line of
the head and cut around.
5. Roll the plate below the arms to form the
skirt, Fig. b. Hold it in place with a paper clip.
6. Fold the upper half of the plate down, behind the clipped side of the skirt. The head and
arms will stand up straight.
7. Cut yellow paper stars and a circle halo.
8. Glue a star to each hand and the halo to the
back of the head.
9. Draw a face on the head with a crayon or
marker.

Hanging Banner

Candy canes and silver balls,
Wreaths and Christmas cheer.
This hanging banner says it all,
This happy time of year.

THINGS YOU NEED—scissors, colored poster board (oaktag), wire coat hanger, colored paper, glue, tape

1. Cut a sheet of colored poster board slightly narrower than the length of a wire coat hanger.
2. Fold a little of the top edge over.
3. Cut six colored paper squares or rectangles to fit on the oaktag.
4. Paste the squares on the oaktag a little away from the folded top edge.
5. Cut Christmas designs from colored paper to fit on the squares.
6. Glue the designs on the squares.
7. Fold the folded top edge over the bottom of a wire coat hanger and tape in place at the back.
8. Hang on a door or wall.

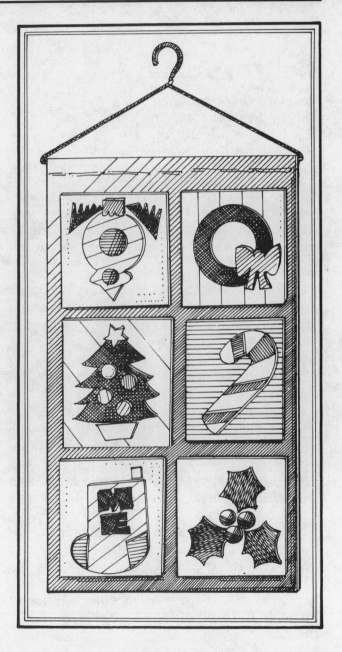

Nativity Family

Years ago in Bethlehem,
On one December morn,
A star shone brightly as a gem,
Where Jesus Christ was born.

THINGS YOU NEED — scissors, colored paper, cardboard bathroom tissue tubes, tape, glue, Ping-Pong balls, white tissue paper, colored markers, quart-sized milk carton, poster paint, kitchen cleanser, brush, tube macaroni, cotton

1. Cut colored paper as high as bathroom tissue tubes. The paper should be long enough to wrap around the tubes plus a little extra. Cut blue for Mary, brown for Joseph, red, orange and yellow for the Three Kings.
2. Roll the paper around the tubes, Fig. a. Tape in place, Fig. b.
3. Cut blue and brown paper rectangles for Mary's and Joseph's capes. Make them as high as the tube but not large enough to wrap around completely.
4. Roll the capes around the tops of the tubes with the bottom edge flaring out, Fig. c. Tape or glue in place.
5. Cut a heart for Mary and a pointed bar for Joseph. Glue to the front of the capes, Fig. c.
6. Make the capes of the Three Kings the same way as you did Mary's and Joseph's, except they should be shorter. Glue a different shape to the front of each cape, Fig. d.

7. Glue a paper gift below each King's cape.
8. Cut several squares of white tissue paper large enough to wrap around a Ping-Pong ball plus a little extra.
9. Place the Ping-Pong ball in the center of the stacked sheets of paper, Fig. e. Bring the sides up over the ball and twist them together, Fig. f.
10. Draw a face and hair for each figure on a wrapped Ping-Pong ball with a marker.
11. Glue a head to the top of each figure with the ends of the tissue tucked inside the tube, Fig. g.
12. Glue a paper ring to the back of Mary's and Joseph's heads for a halo. Glue a crown to the front of each King's head.
*13. Cut a tube in half. Use one half for the baby Jesus. Cover the tube with paper and add a head with a smiling face.
*14. Cut away the bottom of a quart-sized milk carton for the manger. Paint it with poster paint which has a little cleanser added. The cleanser helps the paint stick to the carton.
15. Cut slits into two pieces of paper for straw. Put both in the manger, with Jesus between them.
16. Glue four macaroni legs to the other half of the cut tube to make a lamb, Fig. h.
17. Draw a lamb's face on a covered Ping-Pong ball with a marker. Glue the head to one end of the tube, Fig. h.
18. Glue cotton on the tube for the lamb's wool, Fig. i.

a

b

c

d

e

f

g

h

i

Table Top Tree

Take a sheet of paper
and you will quickly see
That with some folds and cutting
It becomes a Christmas tree.

THINGS YOU NEED—pencil, large sheet of green paper, ruler, tape, scissors, glue, red and yellow paper

1. Mark the center point on one long side of a sheet of green paper; see arrow in Fig. a.
2. Draw lines with a pencil and ruler from the center point out to the sides and bottom; study lines in Fig. a.
3. Fold the paper along all drawn lines. All folds should be made on the same side of the paper.
4. Roll the paper into a cone, with the center point at the top and folds out, Fig. b. Tape in place.
5. Trim the bottom edge so the cone stands straight.
6. Untape the cone.
7. Make four angled cuts into each folded side. All cuts point down from the center point, arrows in Fig. c.
8. Retape the cone, Fig. d.
9. Lift up all the V shaped cuts slightly.
10. Glue red paper circles on the tree. Glue a yellow star to the top.

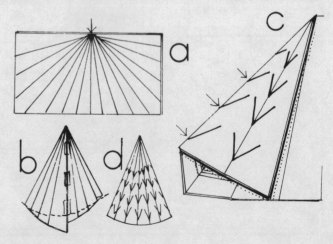

Holly Garland

Make the room look jolly,
With this wreath of holly.

THINGS YOU NEED—pencil, tracing paper, scissors, green paper, crayon or marker, roll of green crepe paper ribbon, stapler

1. Trace the leaf shape from this book on tracing paper or any lightweight paper.
2. Cut out the tracing and use it as a pattern.
3. Trace around the pattern on green paper. Make several leaf shapes.
4. Cut out all the traced leaves.
5. Draw a vein design on each leaf with a crayon or marker.
6. Unwind a roll of green crepe paper ribbon.
7. Staple the leaves to the crepe paper.
8. String the garland on a stair bannister, fireplace mantle, or a table.

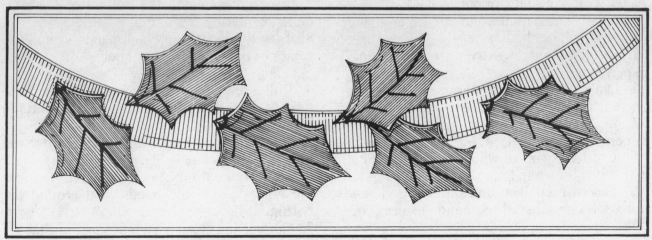

Mr. and Mrs. S. Claus

It's time to start cleaning because,
Your room should be perfect, no flaws,
It's that time of year,
Their arrival is near,
It's the missus and old Santa Claus.

THINGS YOU NEED—scissors, colored paper, two round cardboard containers (salt, oatmeal, cleanser, etc.), tape, pencil, glue, crayons or markers, paper punch, white tissue paper, elastic band, cotton, pom-pom

1. Cut pieces of red paper as high as the round containers. They should be long enough to wrap around the containers plus a little extra.
2. Wrap the paper around each container and tape, Fig. a.
3. Trace one end of each container on red paper with a pencil. Cut out circles.
4. Glue a circle to one end of each container. This end will be the top.
5. Cut two narrow strips of skin-colored paper.
6. Draw a face in the center of each strip with crayons or markers.
7. Wrap the strips around the top of the containers and tape in place, Fig. b.
8. Cut two strips of white paper for the hair. Cut slits along one long side of each, Fig. c.
9. Cut two red arms and skin-colored hands for each container. Tape hands to arm ends, Fig. d.

10. Glue the hair around the faces. Glue the arms to both sides of the containers, Fig. e.

A. Mrs. Claus
1. Cut a strip of white paper for the apron. Cut one long side scalloped. Punch a hole in each scalloped section with a paper punch.
2. Glue the apron to the container, Fig. f. Cut out and glue a white collar under the face.
3. Cut a white tissue paper circle that is much larger than the top of the container, Fig. g.
4. Attach the circle to the container above the face with an elastic band, Fig. h.

B. Santa Claus
1. Cut a long piece of black paper for the boots. Cut a small V into the center.
2. Tape the paper to the bottom of the container, centering the V, Fig. i.
3. Tape a thin strip of black paper around the center of the container for a belt. Add a yellow buckle to the front, Fig. i.
4. Roll a red cone large enough to fit over the top of the container, tape in place and trim the edges, Fig. j.
5. Place the cone, with a pom-pom glued to the top, on Santa's head, Fig. k.
6. Glue on a cotton beard. Glue cotton above the boots, above the hands, and around the bottom of the cone, Fig. k.
7. Cut out and glue on a white paper mustache.

Special Occasion Parties

The year is filled with special occasions which are neither birthdays nor holidays but which are great fun to celebrate. Like the Mad Hatter's tea party in "Alice in Wonderland," held for anyone having an unbirthday, you too can turn any day from the last day of school to a new baby in the family into a time for celebration.

Mother's Day Party

This special day, devoted to mothers, comes in May. In many parts of the country this is a month of warm, sunny days when spring flowers bloom. Why not surprise your mother with a family party? Bake a party cake that looks like a flower garden and make special "Mom" cupcakes too. Since no party is complete without a special gift, give your mom a handmade lacy trinket box. Make this once-a-year celebration a day she will always remember.

May Basket Cake

A tisket, a tasket,
For mom, a May basket.

THINGS YOU NEED — cake mix, round cake pan, yellow frosting mix, plastic knife, three store-bought cupcakes, gel icings in tubes.

* 1. Bake a cake in a round pan. Follow package directions. Remove from the pan and let cool.
2. Mix the frosting according to package directions. Frost the cake with a plastic knife.
3. Decorate the cake with gel icings in tubes. Make a flower basket design, similar to the one shown in the drawing.
4. Decorate three frosted cupcakes with gel icing in a tube to spell M O M.

Tuna Treats and Mocha Cocoa

1. Mix tuna fish with mayonnaise and sweet pickle relish.

*2. Trim away the crusts of several slices of bread. Cut each slice into thirds. Spread the tuna mixture on half the bread pieces and cover with the other half for little finger sandwiches.

3. Make hot cocoa and add a half a teaspoon of instant, decaffeinated coffee to each cup. Mix. Float tiny marshmallows sprinkled with cinnamon on the top.

Lacy Trinket Box

Decorate a box with lace,
And watch the smile on your mom's face.

THINGS YOU NEED — scissors, ribbons and trims, small box with cover, glue

1. Cut lengths of ribbon and trim to fit across the cover of the box.

2. Glue them to the cover, close to each other.

3. Cut ribbons and trims long enough to wrap around the sides of the box and cover. Place the cover on the box before glueing the trims in place.

Father's Day Party

Fathers also have a special day. It arrives almost at the same time summer makes its appearance. Trees are in bloom all across the country. It is a time to go outdoors and enjoy a walk in the woods or at the beach.

Get formal this Father's Day and dress up for the occasion. Serve hefty triple-decker sandwiches made for a king or a hungry dad. Give him a handy workshop organizer he can really use. End the celebration with a funny necktie cake.

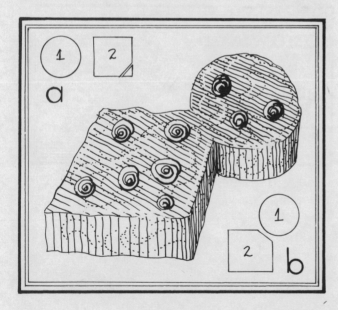

Necktie Cake

When you serve this necktie cake,
A second slice your dad will take.

THINGS YOU NEED—cake mix, round and square cake pans, cookie sheet, aluminum foil, plastic knife, frosting mix, gel icing in a tube

*1. Bake a cake in a round and a square cake pan. Follow package directions. Remove from the pans and let cool.
2. Cover a cookie sheet with aluminum foil.
3. Trim away one corner from the square cake, Fig. a.
4. Arrange the cakes on the cookie sheet with the cut corner of the square cake touching the round cake, Fig. b.
5. Mix the frosting according to package directions. Frost the cake with a plastic knife.
6. Make polka dots with gel icing in a tube.

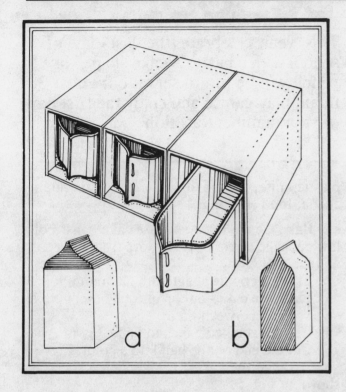

Workshop Organizer

This set of drawers just can't be beat,
To keep dad's tools so safe and neat.

THINGS YOU NEED — three quart-sized milk cartons, stapler, scissors, three half-gallon milk cartons, poster paint, brush, kitchen cleanser, glue

1. Staple the open end of three quart-sized milk cartons closed with a stapler.
2. Cut away the top of three half-gallon cartons; see shaded area in Fig. a.
3. Cut away one side of each quart-sized carton, to the peak; see shaded area in Fig. b.
4. Paint the outer sides of all cartons with poster paint that has a little kitchen cleanser added to it. The cleanser will make the paint stick better.
5. Glue the sides of the three half-gallon cartons together.
6. Slip the quart-sized cartons into the half-gallon cartons. The peaked side will serve as a handle.

Chocolate Float and King-Sized Club Sandwiches

1. Mix chocolate syrup with a little milk in a glass. Fill the glass almost to the top with club soda.
2. Add a scoop of ice cream to make a float.
3. Make daddy-sized sandwiches with four slices of bread filled with cheese, meat slices, lettuce, and tomatoes.

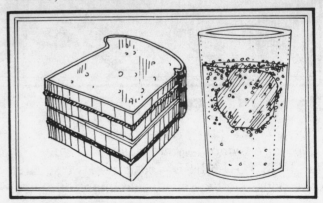

Last Day Of School Party

School is out and you have summer vacation to look forward to. Sleeping late, warm weather, swimming, and no homework are just some of the highlights.

This year celebrate the last day of school with a party. A cake shaped like a pencil will be fun to serve to friends. So relax, play games and enjoy the first day of your summer vacation.

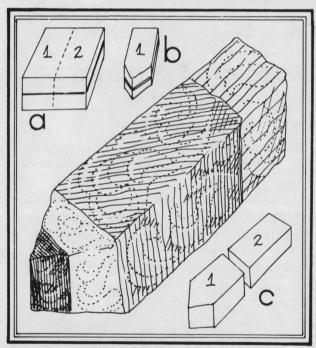

Pencil Cake

A pencil cake's the perfect thing,
"No more school" – your friends will sing.
THINGS YOU NEED—cake mix, two square cake pans, cookie sheet, aluminum foil, jam, plastic knife, two boxes of white frosting mix, cocoa, food coloring

*1. Bake a cake in two square cake pans. Follow package directions. Remove from the pans and let cool.

2. Cover a cookie sheet with aluminum foil.

3. Place the cakes on top of each other with a layer of jam between them.

4. Cut the stacked cakes in half, Fig. a.

5. Cut the end of one half into a point, Fig. b.

6. Arrange the cakes on the cookie sheet as shown in Fig. c.

7. Mix two boxes of frosting mix according to package directions.

8. Add cocoa to a little of the frosting. Use this to frost half of the point of the cake (for the graphite tip) with a plastic knife.

9. Frost the other half of the point white.

10. Add yellow food coloring to the three-quarters of the remaining frosting for the pencil. Add a drop of red to the remaining one-quarter of the frosting.

11. Frost the eraser of the pencil cake with the pink frosting. Frost the remaining cake with the yellow frosting.

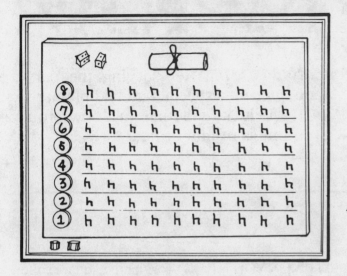

6. To play the game, each player starts at the first circle, grade 1, with a bottle cap. Two dice are rolled by each player, who then moves the number of desks shown on the dice. When you reach the end of a row, go to the first desk of the next row. The first to reach the diploma wins.

Freedom Fondue

1. Cut fruit and pound cake into bite-sized pieces.
*2. Melt a large bag of chocolate bits with a little bit of condensed milk in a pot over a low flame.
3. Spear the fruit and cake with a fork and dip them into the melted chocolate.
4. Serve ice-cold milk.

School Days Game

Throw the dice, don't be afraid,
High rolls move you up a grade.

THINGS YOU NEED — scissors, colored paper, crayons, glue, large sheet of white paper, ruler, plastic bottle caps, dice

1. Cut eight small circles from colored paper. Write a number, from 1 to 8, on each circle with a crayon.
2. Glue the circles on the left side of a large sheet of paper. Start with 1 at the bottom and end with 8 at the top.
3. Draw a line, with a crayon and ruler, going across the paper between every two circles.
4. Draw 10 simple chair shapes in each row.
5. Draw a diploma at the top of the paper.

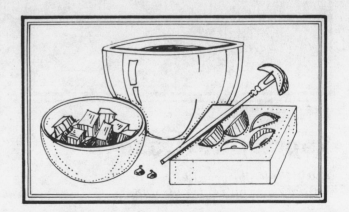

Graduation Day Party

If any member of your family is graduating from school soon, celebrate with a party. Turn the last report card into a cake and present the graduate with his or her own graduation cap (called a mortarboard). After serving the party food, present a special family diploma, to show the lucky graduate just how proud everyone is of him or her.

Report Card Cake

Raise your glasses, make a toast,
To the one you're proud of most.

THINGS YOU NEED — cake mix, square cake pan, metal knife, white frosting mix, plastic knife, gel icing in a tube, ginger ale, plastic champagne glasses

*1. Bake a cake in a square cake pan. Follow package directions. Remove from the pan and let cool.

*2. Cut away the puffy top of the cake with a knife to make it flat.

3. Mix the frosting according to package directions. Frost the cake with a plastic knife.

4. Decorate the top of the cake to look like a report card, using gel icing in a tube.

5. Toast the graduate with ginger ale in plastic champagne glasses. You can add a little strawberry or cherry syrup to the ginger ale.

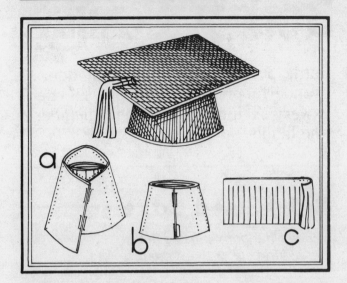

Graduation Cap

Happy is the lucky chap,
Who wears this graduation cap.

THINGS YOU NEED—black paper, plastic tub (margarine, cottage cheese, etc.), tape, scissors, colored tissue paper

1. Roll black paper around a plastic tub which is big enough to fit the graduate's head. Tape in place, Fig. a.
2. Trim away the paper at the top and bottom edges of the tub, Fig. b.
3. Cut a long piece of tissue paper. Cut deep slits into one long side, Fig. c.
4. Roll the paper tightly around itself along the uncut edge for a tassel. Tape in place.
5. Tape the tassel in the center of one side of a large black paper square.
6. Tape the square to the small end of the tub.

Graduation Certificate

Graduate, we'd like to say,
The family's proud of you today.

THINGS YOU NEED—large sheet of white paper, crayons or markers, colored paper, scissors, glue

1. Draw a certificate, similar to the one shown in the drawing, on a large sheet of paper with a crayon or marker. Fill in the dotted line with the correct number and school.
2. Cut a yellow circle with a zigzag edge. Cut two blue ribbon shapes.
3. Glue the ribbons to the circle. Glue the circle and ribbons to the certificate.

Brand New Baby Party

You might just be lucky enough to be getting a new brother or sister. When the baby arrives welcome him or her with a party. Serve tiny cakes and place a paper rattle decoration on the front door. A wonderful present is a hanging mobile. It is very exciting having a new member of the family.

Baby-Sized Cake

A meet-the-baby-party's fun,
Serve little cakes to everyone.

THINGS YOU NEED—cupcake mix, cupcake tins, vanilla frosting mix, plastic knife, shredded coconut, candle, milk, ribbon

1. Bake cupcakes in the cupcake pans. Follow package directions. Remove from the pans and let cool.
2. Mix the frosting according to package directions and frost the top of the cupcakes with a plastic knife.
3. Sprinkle coconut on top of the cupcakes.
4. Place a candle in the center of each.
5. Serve with baby's favorite drink, milk. You can tie a ribbon around the glass.

Rattle Decoration

A baby rattle points the way,
To baby's crib, that's where he'll stay.

THINGS YOU NEED—pencil, colored paper, compass, scissors, glue, crayons or markers, ribbon

1. Draw a rattle shape, similar to the one shown in the drawing, on colored paper. Use a compass for the circles. Cut out.
2. Cut and glue a small white circle in the center of the smaller circle of the rattle shape.
3. Write a welcome message on the larger circle with a crayon or marker.
4. Tie ribbon into a bow around the center bar.

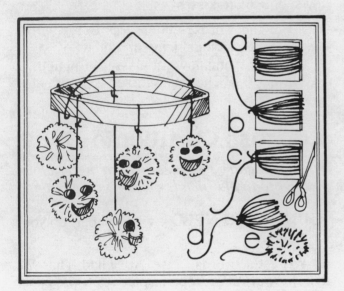

THINGS YOU NEED—scissors, poster board (oaktag), tape, yarn, colored paper or felt, glue

1. Cut a strip from poster board or any other sturdy paper. Make a ring and tape in place.
2. Cut a small square of poster board no longer than your middle finger.
3. Wrap yarn around the poster board square, Fig. a. The more yarn you wrap, the fluffier the pom-pom will be.
4. Tie all the yarn at one end of the square, together with a piece of yarn, Fig. b. One end of the yarn should be longer than the other.
5. Cut through all the yarn at the other end of the square, Fig. c.
6. Remove the yarn and fluff it to form a pom-pom, Figs. d and e.
7. Cut eyes and a mouth from colored paper or felt. Glue them to the pom-poms. Make many pom-poms.
8. Tie the pom-poms to the ring. Tie a length of yarn to the ring to make a hanging.

Fuzzy-Wuzzy Mobile

Make a fuzzy-wuzzy toy,
For the baby girl or boy.

Moving Away Party

Whether it is you or someone you know who is moving, make it a happy time with a party. Invite all of the neighborhood friends for a farewell get-together. Feast on cupcakes and punch. Make a keepsake album that contains all the good neighborhood memories and have a grand day.

THINGS YOU NEED—store-bought frosted cupcakes, gel icing in a tube, punch, marshmallows, chocolate kisses

1. Write the words, "G•O•O•D B•Y," across six cupcakes with gel icing in a tube.
2. Float marshmallows in glasses of punch.
3. Have lots of chocolate kisses on hand.

Address Certificate

When you carry this sheet, you're never alone.
Just write to old friends or call on the phone.

THINGS YOU NEED—white paper, crayons or markers

1. Write the words, "We Are Glad That We Knew You," at the top of a piece of white paper with a crayon or marker.
2. Draw a house on both sides of the paper at the bottom. Draw footprints going from one house to the other.
3. Every guest writes his or her name, address, and telephone number between the houses.

Farewell Snick Snacks

Pack up all your odds and ends,
Then throw a party, invite your friends.

Keepsake Album

A memory book for when you depart,
Reminds you of friends dear to your heart.

THINGS YOU NEED—scissors, cardboard, colored paper, paper punch, pencil, crayons or markers, cord

1. Cut two pieces of cardboard and several sheets of colored paper all the same size.
2. Punch two holes near the edge of one short side of a piece of cardboard with a paper punch. Use this punched cardboard as a pattern to mark where the holes should be on the pieces of paper and the other piece of cardboard.
3. Every guest at the party gets a sheet of paper. They write their names, add photographs, glue on magazine cut-outs that have special meaning, jokes, poems, or their own words. These sheets will go in the book for the person who is leaving.

4. Line up all the sheets between the two pieces of cardboard.
5. Push a length of cord into both holes. Tie the cord into a bow on the front cardboard.
6. Write the words, "Remember Us Always," on the front.

Anniversary Party

Make the wedding bells ring again for your parents by giving them an anniversary party.

Every guest gets a wedding favor and don't forget the bouquet of flowers for your mother.

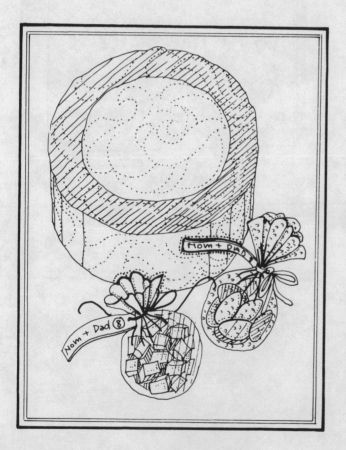

Ring Cake and Favors

"Happy Anniversary,"
Is the perfect song,
When you serve this ring cake
Sing it out strong.

THINGS YOU NEED—cake mix, two round cake pans, white frosting mix, yellow food coloring, plastic knife, scissors, colored paper, paper punch, marker, pastel mints and candy-covered almonds, clear kitchen wrap, yarn

A. Ring Cake
*1. Bake a cake in two round cake pans. Follow package directions. Remove from the pans and let cool.
2. Mix the frosting according to package directions. Add yellow food coloring to one-quarter of the frosting.
3. Spread the frosting between the two cakes with a plastic knife.
4. Frost a ring around the top of the cake with yellow frosting.
5. Frost the rest of the cake with white frosting.

B. Favors

1. Cut strips of colored paper and punch a hole into one end with a paper punch. Write the names of the anniversary couple on the strips with a marker.

2. Place candies on a square of clear kitchen wrap.

3. Tie a length of yarn to each name strip.

Gather the wrap around the candies and tie the wrap closed with the yarn.

Anniversary Bouquet

Make a paper flower bouquet,
For your folks this special day.

THINGS YOU NEED—scissors, colored paper, glue, markers, stapler, plastic drinking straws, tape, plastic bowl or tub (margarine, cottage cheese, etc.), potting soil

1. Cut two different-sized circles for flower shapes from colored paper. Glue the smaller circle on the larger circle. Make a flower for each anniversary year.

2. Write a number on each flower for each anniversary with a marker.

3. Staple each flower to one end of a drinking straw.

4. Cut out leaf shapes from green paper. Tape one or two to each straw.

5. Fill a bowl or tub with potting soil. Push the straws into the soil for a pretty bouquet.

Welcome Home Party

Has someone you really love been gone for a long time and will he or she be coming home soon? If so, then the best present to give is a Welcome Home Party. The first thing this person should see is a large "Welcome Home" sign on the door. Bake a cake for the occasion. Best of all, greet this long-lost person with plenty of hugs and kisses.

Welcome Home Sign

Create a "Welcome Home" sign for the front door. Use crayons or markers on white paper.

Home Sweet Home Cake

Bake and decorate a cake, following the instructions given for the Gingerbread House, page 36.

Love and Kisses

Tell that special person how much you missed him or her. Make a Basket of Hearts following the instructions on page 152.